TIMES *of* REFRESHING

VOLUME 3

BOOKS BY DR. JOE IBOJIE

*Bible-Based Dictionary of Prophetic Symbols
for Every Christian*

The Watchman

Dreams and Visions Volume 1
International Best Seller

Dreams and Visions Volume 2

The Justice of God: Victory in Everyday Living

How to Live the Supernatural Life in the Here and Now
International Best Seller

Illustrated Bible-Based Dictionary of Dream Symbols
International Best Seller

Destined for the Top

Times of Refreshing Volume 1

Times of Refreshing Volume 2

Times of Refreshing Volume 3—**New**

Revelation Training Manual—**New**

How You Can Live an Everyday Supernatural Life—**New**

AVAILABLE FROM CROSS HOUSE BOOKS

TIMES *of* REFRESHING

VOLUME 3

INSPIRATION, PRAYERS, & GOD'S WORD FOR EACH DAY

BISHOP JOE IBOJIE &
PASTOR CYNTHIA IBOJIE

CROSS HOUSE BOOKS
Christian Book Publishers
245 Midstocket Road
Aberdeen
AB15 5PH, UK

"The entrance of Your Word brings light."

ISBN: 978-0-9574782-6-8

For Worldwide Distribution, Printed in U.S.A.

1 2 3 4 5 6 7 / 18 17 16 15 14

To order products by Dr. Joe Ibojie & other Cross House Books, contact sales@crosshousebooks.co.uk.

Other correspondence: info@crosshousebooks.co.uk.

Visit www.crosshousebooks.co.uk.

Introduction

WE are pleased to present this third volume filled with inspiration, love, and hope. Being in ministry together, we appreciate the close relationships we have with others and each other—friendships made in Heaven.

> *As iron sharpens iron, so a friend sharpens a friend* (Proverbs 27:17 NLT).

As such, we have poured over each Scripture for each day and have prayerfully contemplated each of the insights we received. Then we inserted some questions to prompt you to delve into your inner being, searching and discovering truths that the Lord has for you—nuggets of His love and wisdom.

Only He can truly guide you on your way toward your destiny—fulfilling your dreams and visions. We are privileged and honored to be part of His plan by sharing what He has for you through us.

> *Listen, dear friends, to God's truth, bend your ears to what I tell you. I'm chewing on the morsel of a proverb; I'll let you in on the sweet old truths, Stories we heard from our fathers, counsel we learned at our mother's knee. **We're not keeping this to ourselves, we're passing it along to the next generation—God's fame and fortune, the marvelous things he has done*** (Psalm 78:1-4 The Message).

We joyfully pass along to you the glorious message of God's love and grace and mercy. May you grow in faith each and every day of every New Year!

I Was Thinking of You

I will praise you, Lord, among the nations; I will sing of you among the peoples (Psalm 57:9).

THIS morning on this first day of the year I was thinking and thanking God for allowing our paths to cross. We should thank God for the many people He has allowed into our lives—each bring value and enrichment to the meaning of life.

Over the course of last year, you probably noticed many changes in your life. Things do change! Only one thing is constant—God—He is dependable and He never fails! As for me, I will continue to stand in prayer for the saints of God until they are fully established in God's purpose for their lives. As you reflect on 2013, be assured His grace will abound and will turn all challenges to positive actions and victories in 2014.

In 2014, Acts 2 will play out in your life; all that belongs to you will *gather* to you; you will hear pleasant *sounds from heaven*; your household will be *filled* with God; the power of God will overshadow and energize you; you will manifest your hidden potentials, and the people will see and be amazed and give glory to God. May this year be your year of gathering things together!

Take Away for Today

1. You may have already set your goals for the New Year. If not, write them today. Include what you hope to accomplish in your spiritual life, your family circumstances, your career, and your education.

_____

_____

Reading the Bible in a Year: Genesis 1-2 and Matthew 1.

CONTEND FOR YOUR VISION

Fight the good fight of the faith. Take hold of the eternal life to which you were called when you made your good confession in the presence of many witnesses (1 Timothy 6:12).

PAUL advised his spiritual son, Timothy, to contend for his call. I supposed Paul more than anyone else is better placed to say this because he was well experienced in the vicissitudes of life on earth. Later he said of himself, *"I have fought the good fight, I have finished the race, I have kept the faith"* (2 Tim. 4:7). This is all that counts.

Dreams are precious! Never give up on your dream! If people gave up on you and your dream, it is because they do not know the power of prayers. I believe in prayers, and therefore I believe in you! Remember, if failure was not a possibility, success has no value. Though the events of your life make the fabric of who you are and how you act and react, but your final outcome is in God's hand. Life may give you a scar, but the vision still stands and has no expiry date. With God you will not fail.

Take Away for Today

1. How many dreams have you put on the shelf because others have discouraged you?

2. Is it time for you to resurrect that long-range, God-given vision you have for your life?

3. What first steps can you take today to revive your aspirations?

_____

_____

DIVINE FORCES WILL
FIGHT YOUR BATTLES

Then GOD expanded the vision to include four blacksmiths. I asked, "And what are these all about?" He said, "Since the 'horns' scattered Judah so badly that no one had any hope left, these blacksmiths have arrived to combat the horns. They'll dehorn the godless nations who used their horns to scatter Judah to the four winds" (Zechariah 1:20-21 The Message).

THE Bible says God *"expanded the vision"* for the prophet Zechariah to include His four forces to "dehorn" the enemies that had lifted their horns against Israel! From now on, you can raise up your head, as God fights your battles. Whenever you have revelation of the plans of the enemy of your soul, ask God to expand your vision to include His counteracting forces to bring justice to your situation.

One of the basic revelatory principles to remember is that usually God first reveals the strategy of the enemy *for information,* and then reveals His superior plans for *action and divine justice.* Therefore oblige yourself of all available resources in God's arsenal as the Bible says, *"take everything the Master has set out for you, well-made weapons of the best materials. And put them to use so you will be able to stand up to everything the Devil throws your way"* (Eph. 6:10-11 The Message).

Take Away for Today

1. What do you think "combat the horns" means?

2. How can you allow God to "dehorn" the enemies in your life?

3. Do you believe that God wants to fight your battles?

THE POWER OF DESTINY

*David said to Solomon: "My son, I had it in my heart to build a house for the Name of the LORD my God. **But this word of the LORD came to me:** 'You have shed much blood and have fought many wars. You are not to build a house for my Name, because you have shed much blood on the earth in my sight. But you will have a son who will be a man of peace and rest.... He is the one who will build a house for my Name"* (1 Chronicles 22:6-10).

ALTHOUGH the Lord loved David, He could not allow Him to build His house because of all the bloodshed. God chose Solomon to build the Temple and promised him great things. How comforting it must have been for David to know his son would be blessed abundantly by God. How relieved for David to know the God would not hold the bloodshed against his son. We can be just as comforted and relieved knowing that God loves our natural children more than we ever could—and will watch over them. This is the heritage of the righteous: *"All your children will be taught by the LORD, and great will be their peace"* (Isa. 54:13-15). May the power of destiny propel our children to their rightful places and purposes in God.

Take Away for Today

1. Have you been comforted and relieved reading this Scripture passage?

2. When the time comes, can you slip from this life to the next knowing that God will take care of your family to the best of His Almighty ability?

THE PRIVILEGE
OF BEING GOD'S SERVANT

*But when God, who **set me apart** from birth, and **called me**
by his grace, was **pleased to reveal** his Son in me so that I
might preach him among the Gentiles...* (Galatians 1:15-16).

PAUL said God set him apart from birth, and called him by His
grace; God was pleased to reveal His Son in Paul so that he might
preach Him among the people. This is the story of how God helped
Paul! Like Paul you too have been:

- Set apart by Him from *birth*
- Called by *grace*
- Justified by *faith*
- Empowered by *revelation* of His Son already in you.

Be encouraged; you will not fail because by His strength you too
will succeed!

Take Away for Today

1. Do you consider serving God a privilege or a chore?

2. Do you believe that God chose you before you were
   even born to serve Him?

3. How real to you is the fact Jesus lives within you?

_____

_____

_____

You Can't Give Up Now

But as for me, my feet had almost slipped; I had nearly lost my foothold. ...till I entered the sanctuary of God; then I understood their final destiny (Psalm 73:2,17).

As long as we live in our earthen vessels, we will come across situations that tend to suggest we cannot make it to the end—but the Lord is our Shepherd and He leads us because we are the sheep of His pasture! The palmist was once in a difficult situation and thought he was going lose everything—but God showed up for him and he came to divine realization. In contemporary terms we can say, "I almost gave up...but see what the Lord has done to save me!" Give the Lord His glory in whatever you are going through. He will surely show up!

Take Away for Today

1. Have you ever felt like the psalmist...that you almost lost your foothold on life?

2. Have often do you turn to God to lead you out of a difficult situation? Is it often enough?

A BOOK OF REMEMBRANCE

*Then those who feared the LORD **spoke to one another,** and **the LORD listened** and heard them; so a **book of remembrance** was written before Him for those who fear the LORD and who **meditate on His name*** (Malachi 3:16 NKJV).

A Book of Remembrance is one of the books of heaven! *Praise* is to speak about Him to each other; *worship* is to think of His nature and honor Him. Today, above all else, praise and worship Him and continue to keep and maintain your name in this great book! God inhabits the praises of His people and we enter His court with praise. Worship has many facets but very often it is an art of warfare to win our battles!

Take Away for Today

1. What do you think is contained in the book of remembrance about you?
2. How often do you meditate on His name?
3. How often do you speak to others about Him?

Reading the Bible in a Year: Genesis 18-19 and Matthew 6.

PRAYER DAY

P RAY throughout the day using the following points:

1. The heavens will be open over you; *"the heavens were opened and I saw visions of God...the word of the Lord came...the hand of the Lord was on him"* (see Ezekiel 1:1-3).

2. The Lord will stretch forth His hands to heal and perform miraculous signs and wonder (see Acts 4:27-31).

3. Pray for the miracle of divine provision, *"I will fill this valley with pools of water. You will see neither wind nor rain, yet this valley will be filled with water, and you, your cattle and your other animals will drink"* (see 2 Kings 3:16-17).

4. Pray for unity in the Body of Christ and your city, wherever you may be.

Take Away for Today

1. What do you usually focus on when you pray?

2. Does having a Scripture passage help you to concentrate more on your time with God in prayer?

3. Is there a specific urgent need for unity in the Body of Christ in your church?

SPEAK—I'M READY TO LISTEN

..."Speak. I'm your servant, ready to listen"
(1 Samuel 3:10 The Message).

THIS encounter with God revealed in First Samuel 3 was the beginning of all the incredible revelations Samuel received in his life. There is always a beginning! But Samuel needed Eli to teach him when he did not know the voice of the Lord. This is why we must not despise the days of small beginnings.

Start today, this is your revelatory journey with God and the same will be true of you. When you are ready to listen and you are in the right place in God, God will reveal Himself by His word. No matter the geography of your birth and the circumstance of your life, may God reveal and prove Himself strong in your life through His word!

Take Away for Today

1. Are you God's servant?
2. Are you ready to listen when He speaks to you?
3. Have you heard His voice while meditating in His Word—the Bible?

WORSHIP AS AN ART OF WARFARE

As they began to sing and praise, the Lord set ambushes against the men of Ammon and Moab and Mount Seir who were invading Judah, and they were defeated (2 Chronicles 20:22).

OUR worship with singing and praising and also our sacrifices to God will bring His aid to us. *"While Samuel was sacrificing the burnt offering, the Philistines drew near to engage Israel in battle. But that day the Lord thundered against the Philistines and threw them into such a panic"* (1 Sam. 7:10). It was a panic sent by God. In both instances as the ones who loved God raised their voices in worship, the Lord fought their battles! Don't die in silence! Speak God's word to your situation, praise Him and get out of your difficulties and worship Him in the midst of your battles.

Take Away for Today

1. Do you routinely use worship of the Lord to defeat your challenges and enemies?
2. What type of worship do you enjoy most?
3. Are you attuned to the depth of your worship—your sincerity of your praises?

_____

_____

_____

GOOD PEOPLE WILL FLOURISH LIKE PALM TREES

The sight of my critics going down is still fresh, the rout of my malicious detractors. My ears are filled with the sounds of promise: "Good people will prosper like palm trees, grow tall like Lebanon cedars; transplanted to GOD's courtyard, they'll grow tall in the presence of God, lithe and green, virile still in old age" (Psalm 92:10-12 The Message).

NOTICE the duality of God's victory; restoration of what was lost and reposition for present and future advantage plus the ruin of those who wanted to plunder you and the lingering echo of the sound of their downfall. May these promises from God be your portion in life! You will flourish like the palm tree and grow like the cedar of Lebanon!

Take Away for Today

1. Write in your own words what the Lord promises to "Good people."

2. Do you consider yourself to be a good person? Are you accepting these promises as your own?

Reading the Bible in a Year: Genesis 27-28 and Matthew 9:18-38.

YOUR PRAYERS MAKE THE DIFFERENCE

As for me, far be it from me that I should sin against the Lord by failing to pray for you. And I will teach you the way that is good and right (1 Samuel 12:23).

SAMUEL says that it is actually a sin against the Lord if we don't pray for others. Perhaps Samuel remembered the words of his mentor, priest Eli: *"If one person sins against another, God may mediate for the offender; but if anyone sins against the LORD, who will intercede for them?"* (1 Samuel 2:25). If you have the power and opportunity to pray for someone and failed to do so, it is not just a mere decision but a grave sin against God Himself. As we are loved and cared for by our heavenly Father, may we love and care for and pray for those with whom He has surrounded us.

Take Away for Today

1. Do you daily pray for others?
2. Do you daily love and care for others?
3. Does this attention for others come naturally or do you have to make a concerted effort to do so?

YOUR VICTORY IS ASSURED

Jonathan said to his young armor-bearer...Perhaps the LORD will act in our behalf. Nothing can hinder the LORD from saving, whether by many or by few (1 Samuel 14:6).

IT does not matter the strength of the enemy—your victory is assured! Truly the Lord can save by many or by few. It means also the strength of the enemy has no value in deciding the outcome of a challenge. The battle belongs to God.

Take Away for Today

1. Is your victory settled in your mind?
2. Have you accepted that the Lord is willing and able to battle for you?
3. How much confidence do you have in the Lord to act on your behalf?

AN END TO MISERY

Help me, Lord my God; save me according to your unfailing love. Let them know that it is your hand, that you, Lord, have done it (Psalm 109:26).

MISERY is any form of great unhappiness or extreme distress; but God promises to put an end to misery in your life! Why? Because you have been translated to His marvelous light and infinite joy. May this be your testimony!

Take Away for Today

1. What misery have you suffered recently? Did you overcome it? How?
2. What other Scripture passages promise you God's light, peace, and joy?
3. In what ways has God revealed his unfailing love for you?

THE TRUTH HAS POWER

Then you will know the truth, and the truth will set you free
(John 8:32).

ALWAYS choose the path of truth—no matter what it seems—and no limitation can hold you back. Then you will be free indeed! Free to be your best; free to be your true and original self as designed by God. There lies your power for victory! As you stick with the truth, you are blessed and your breakthrough is assured and at hand!

Take Away for Today

1. What does it mean to you to be set free?
2. What is holding you captive that you have yet to seek the truth and be set free?
3. Do you purposefully walk on the "path of truth," or do you routinely take detours?

LET IT FLOW

*On the last and greatest day of the festival, Jesus stood and said in a loud voice, **"Let anyone who is thirsty come to me and drink.** Whoever believes in me, as Scripture has said, **rivers of living water will flow from within them."** By this he meant the Spirit, whom those who believed in him were later to receive. Up to that time the Spirit had not been given, since Jesus had not yet been glorified* (John 7:37-39).

TODAY remember you have a well of inexhaustible flow of refreshing and living water within you to keep you from becoming stagnant. So let it flow to whoever may come near you today. Yes, you are source of refreshment in this arid land of life filled with great challenges; never forget this. You will make a wonderful difference in somebody's life!

Take Away for Today

1. Have you felt rivers of living water flowing from you? Often? Seldom?

2. What can you do today to ensure that living water flows from you onto others?

3. Can you feel the Spirit living within you? Have you given Him a place?

MAKE GLAD THE CITY OF GOD

There is a river whose streams make glad the city of God, the holy place where the Most High dwells. God is within her, she will not fall; God will help her at break of day (Psalm 46:4-5).

R EMEMBER this always, God is within you, and His stream will make glad your life. You will find God and His help awaits you at the break of every new day! This is a phrase of reassurance! As indeed, the beginning of this psalm says, *"Therefore we will not fear, though the earth gives way and the mountains fall into the heart of the sea, though its waters roar and foam and the mountains quake with their surging"* (Psalm 46:2-3). You will not fail, "as surely as the sun rises, he will appear" on your behalf.

Take Away for Today

1.   Do you seek God every morning? Every evening? Throughout the day?

2.   How comforting is it to know He wants you to seek Him and that He has promised you will find Him?

3.   Do you realize that you need not seek any further than within your very being?

Reading the Bible in a Year: Genesis 41 and Matthew 13:1-32.

TRUST IN THE LORD

*Trust in the **LORD** with all your heart and lean not on your own understanding; in all your ways submit to him, and he will make your paths straight* (Proverbs 3:5-6).

LET the anchor of your hope be on the solid rock of the Ancient of Days! Then you are assured of easy access to your destiny because He will make your path straight. This passage in Proverbs 3 means to rely on God or to have confidence in God. You can depend on God because He never fails us. Be blessed with this truth—those who put their trust in God will never be disappointed.

Take Away for Today

1. Who or what do you trust in more than God?
2. Have you submitted yourself totally to Him?
3. Have you been walking on the straight path that He paved for you?

FIGHT THE LORD'S BATTLE!

*...The LORD your God will certainly make a lasting dynasty for my lord, because **you fight the LORD's battles,** and no wrongdoing will be found in you as long as you live...*
(1 Samuel 25:28-31).

GOD said to Jeremiah, *"You are My battle-ax and weapons of war: For with you I will break the nation in pieces; with you I will destroy kingdoms; with you I will break in pieces the horse and its rider; with you I will break in pieces the chariot and its rider"* (Jeremiah 51:20-21). A person can become God's weapon of battle; that is what it means to "fight the Lord's battles." Be blessed with the prayers of Abigail (Nabal's wife) found in First Samuel 25:28-3. This was her prayer for David and my prayers for you today:

- The Lord will fight your battles and establish your destiny.
- Your life will be "bound securely in the bundle of the living."
- The lives of your enemies will be hurled away as from the pocket of a sling.
- You will fight the Lord's battles and be blessed.

Take Away for Today

1. When is the last time you prayed such an earnest prayer to God?

2. Do your prayers tend to be the same drone every time?

3. What does it mean to you to know that your life has been bound securely in the bundle of the living?

Reading the Bible in a Year: Genesis 44-45 and Matthew 14:1-21.

A DESTINY HELPER

Now the Lord God said, It is not good (sufficient, satisfactory)
that the man should be alone; I will make him a helper (suitable,
adapted, complementary) for him (Genesis 2:18 AMP).

GENESIS 2:18 tells us what God said concerning finding a wife for Adam; but today He is saying this concerning every area of your life. It is His benevolence and plan for you that a destiny helper will come your way this day. A destiny helper is one who facilitates the agenda of God to bring about the fulfillment of your destiny. You are never alone in God! You will not lack a helper in life who is sufficient, satisfactory, suitably adapted, and complementary.

Take Away for Today

1. Have others helped you through tough times?
2. Has a family member stuck by you through a health issue?
3. Did a co-worker assist you with a new technique or procedure?

VICTORY WHEREVER YOU GO

...The Lord gave David victory wherever he went
(2 Samuel 8:6,14).

TO experience victory is splendid and any victory is worthy of celebration. Many people experience victory once in a while, but God gave David victory wherever he went! This is my prayer for you today—that you will have victory wherever you go. David fought many wars and the Lord gave him the victory (see also 1 Chron. 18:6). As God did for David, so He will do for you! You will live a life of victories.

Take Away for Today

1. Do you believe that God loves you as much as He loved David, and so will provide you victories as well?

2. How many wars have you fought—at home, at work, in your mind—that God has given you victory?

_____

_____

_____

TRUE COMMITMENT

David asked, "Is there anyone still left of the house of Saul to whom I can show kindness for Jonathan's sake?" (2 Samuel 9:1)

DAVID was now established as king; Saul and Jonathan were dead and there was no physical evidence to bind him to his secret oath with Jonathan. But David chose to show true commitment by standing by his secret oath with Jonathan. Often the choice is ours! It does matter what people see on the outside; but what counts is having a right standing with God, who sees what is done in secret. Today show true commitment no matter what.

Take Away for Today

1. David chose the ethical, righteous, and moral thing to do. Do you make the right choices?
2. Do you choose to show kindness whenever possible?

_____

_____

_____

FROM LO DEBAR TO THE KING'S TABLE

So King David had him brought from Lo Debar...So Mephibosheth ate at David's table like one of the king's sons (2 Samuel 9:5,11).

A great transformation came to Mephibosheth from the most unexpected quarters! It was a radical shift in his circumstance. Because of the kindness of David, Jonathan's son, Mephibosheth, went from the place of dejection, misery, and ardent poverty to a place of affluence, honor, and power all in a day. Such is what God can do in the life of those who love Him. As long as it depends on you, show someone kindness today. Your time of promotion has come!

Take Away for Today

1. How do you think Mephibosheth felt when he realized King David wanted him to live as one of his sons?

2. How do you feel realizing that the King of kings wants you to live as one of His children?

COVENANT BY SACRIFICE

Gather My saints together to Me, those who have made a covenant with Me by sacrifice (Psalm 50:5 NKJV).

THIS is how to rise above your circumstance, taking a step of faith and thinking of what you will forsake for the benefit of what you consider more valuable—seeking the ways of God. Be counted in the number of His saints! *"Be generous: Invest in acts of charity. Charity yields high returns"* (Eccl. 11:1 The Message). God wants to commune with those who made covenant with Him by sacrificing what is truly less valuable (anything else) to come into the fellowship of His presence (the value and the essence of life on earth). Your reward is sure!

Take Away for Today

1. Do you continually take steps of faith forward?
2. Do you continually seek the ways and will of God for your life?
3. How genuinely generous are you?

_____

_____

_____

A TWO-DAY FAST

I encourage to you embrace a two-day fast using the following Scriptures to guide and comfort you. I believe that things will shift in your favor! Meditate and pray along the following verses:

> *Therefore I also, after I heard of your faith in the Lord Jesus and your love for all the saints, do not cease to give thanks for you, making mention of you in my prayers: that the God of our Lord Jesus Christ, the Father of glory, may give to you the spirit of wisdom and revelation in the knowledge of Him...* (see Eph. 1:15-22 NKJV).

> *...always laboring fervently for you in prayers, that you may stand perfect and complete in all the will of God* (see Col. 4:12 NKJV).

> *...God gave them knowledge and skill in all literature and wisdom; and Daniel had understanding in all visions and dreams* (Dan. 1:17; see Dan. 5:12).

Take Away for Today

1. What does a fast mean to you?
2. What are the advantages of fasting?
3. Which of the Scripture passages listed seems to be the most motivating? Comforting?

OUT OF THE EATER, SOMETHING TO EAT

"Out of the eater, something to eat; out of the strong, something sweet..." (Judges 14:14).

THIS was the riddle of Samson, a man anointed with extraordinary strength from heaven. Life is full of riddles and it takes wisdom from heaven to unravel the riddle of the mundane things of our daily living. Samson spoke the above riddle out of the abundance of the spirit of might that rested upon him. It takes patience and due diligence to uncover the hidden gold in many of life's difficult situations.

This is my prayer for you: Whatever has resisted you before will become your sweetness and springboard; and whatever wants to eat you up will become food for you! Today you will get divine insight and understanding beyond your expectations! The truth you know will set you free! Wisdom is the principal thing; get some understanding.

Take Away for Today

1. Do you accept this prayer?
2. Do you agree that wisdom and understanding will set you free?

A FAMILY OF DISTINCTION

*Lamech married two wives—Adah and Zillah. To Adah was born a baby named Jabal. He became **the first of the cattlemen** and those living in tents. His brother's name was Jubal, **the first musician—the inventor of the harp and flute.** To Lamech's other wife, Zillah, was born Tubal- cain. He opened **the first foundry forging instruments** of bronze and iron* (Genesis 4:19-22 The Living Bible).

L AMECH'S family was unique and special! Without the benefit of precedence, they distinguished themselves through creativity and excellence. I don't know the prevailing circumstance of their lives, but they became the first to invent or create and the first to venture into many aspects of human life on earth. Well, I may not know your prevailing circumstance either, but may this anointing be upon your family! As the Bible says, *"I* [God] *will provide for them* [you and your family] *a land renowned for its crops"* (Ezekiel 34:29a).

Take Away for Today

1. Have you made it your desire to make your family one of distinction?

2. If your family tree is more infamous than famous, what can you do to turn the next generation around?

LIFTED UP BY THE FLOOD

...as the waters increased they lifted the ark high above the earth (Genesis 7:17).

MANY people have great potentials hidden deep inside of them; and unless the challenges of life arise to reveal these great potentials, they may never be revealed. Without the waters of the flood, the Noah's ark would never have fulfilled its purpose—destiny. May whatever you are facing right now lift you up toward your destiny!

Take Away for Today

1. How easy is it for you to see the silver lining during your dark, stormy days?

2. When challenges seem to flood over you, is that when you get out your life raft and ride the waves?

THE WISDOM OF GOD

*Now David had been told, "Ahithophel is among the conspirators with Absalom." So **David prayed,** "LORD, turn Ahithophel's counsel into foolishness" (2 Samuel 15:31).*

D AVID prayed that Ahithophel's gift would be turned into foolishness, and God granted his request. Any gift from God not used for godly purposes becomes perverted and may be frustrated by God. To use the power of God in your life outside the purposes of God, just because you can use it, is spiritual cockiness. Instead, when troubles and turmoil seem to loom heavy, pray for the wisdom of God to intervene. Because *"There is no wisdom, no insight, no plan that can succeed against the Lord"* (Prov. 21:30). Wisdom of God never fails. With us is the arm of the Lord to fight our battles.

Take Away for Today

1. Prayer is the answer to every question—do you pray without ceasing?

2. Only God's wisdom can overcome evil and foolishness—do you pray for His wisdom?

Your Family Is Chosen by God

Is it not my family God has chosen? Yes, he has made an everlasting covenant with me. His agreement is arranged and guaranteed in every detail. He will ensure my safety and success (2 Samuel 23:5 NLT).

W E are a chosen generation and therefore you are a chosen person and your family is also chosen. I pray that you will be blessed by these words of David, a man anointed by the Most High, Israel's singer of songs. This will also be your testimony.

Take Away for Today

1. Do you have confidence that God has already ensured your safety and success?

2. What do you think David means by "His agreement is arranged and guaranteed in every detail"? Explain.

TURNING POINT

When the angel stretched out his hand to destroy Jerusalem, the LORD relented concerning the disaster and said to the angel who was afflicting the people, "Enough! Withdraw your hand." The angel of the LORD was then at the threshing floor of Araunah the Jebusite (2 Samuel 24:16).

GOD is saying to any destructive agent in your life—"Enough! Withdraw your hand!"

Your days of misery have ended. You have reached the threshing floor of Araunah which is your turning point, the place of exchanging punishment for mercies of God!

Take Away for Today

1. Are you ready to claim this promise of God as your very own?

2. What destructive agents is the Lord ridding from your life right now?

3. What does this turning point mean to you?

_____

_____

_____

THE REWARD OF GIVING

Give, and it will be given to you. A good measure, pressed down, shaken together and running over, will be poured into your lap. For with the measure you use, it will be measured to you (Luke 6:38).

A S the Bible says, it is more blessed to give than to receive. Though the art of receiving is a virtue that eludes many people, the art of giving is a much higher virtue because it is the gateway through which receiving comes! Receiving rests on a tripod of asking (requesting), readiness to receive, and faith in what is received; while giving has many facets including sacrifice, right attitude, faith, good soil, seed, and harvest. Give always and you will never lack!

Take Away for Today

1. Are you better at receiving or giving?
2. Do you always give with the right attitude?
3. Do you always receive with the right attitude?

THE LORD OF BREAKTHROUGH

...As waters break out, the LORD has broken out against my enemies before me... (2 Samuel 5:20).

TRULY, the Lord is the Master of breakthrough! That is why the prophet Micah said *"The One who breaks open the way will go up before them"* (Micah 2:13)—to break through any resistance that may come across your way. He will surely break through for you without fail! Consider the following Scriptures:

> *He thwarts the plans of the crafty, so that their hands achieve no success* (Job 5:12).

> *Declare a holy fast; call a sacred assembly. Summon the elders and all who live in the land to the house of the LORD your God, and cry out to the LORD* (Joel 1:14; see also 2:15-17).

> *Is not this the kind of fasting I have chosen: to loose the chains of injustice and untie the cords of the yoke, to set the oppressed free and break every yoke?* (Isaiah 58:5-12).

> *The One who breaks open the way will go up before them; they will break through the gate and go out. Their King will pass through before them, the LORD at their head* (Micah 2:13).

Take Away for Today

1. Have you experienced a breakthrough in your marriage, finances, career?
2. Have you declared a holy fast lately?
3. Do you depend on the Lord to thwart the plans of the crafty, the evil ones?

A QUIVER FULL OF BLESSINGS

Don't you see that children are GOD's best gift? the fruit of the womb his generous legacy? Like a warrior's fistful of arrows are the children of a vigorous youth. Oh, how blessed are you parents, with your quivers full of children! Your enemies don't stand a chance against you; you'll sweep them right off your doorstep (Psalm 127:3-5 The Message).

CHILDREN are the heritage of the righteous. Perhaps our parent's generation never thought our generation would turn out as good as we have actually done. Children are hidden gems. Despite the struggles of generational divide within every family, be assured that children are God's best gifts and are a generous and wonderful legacy. Today let our prayers focus on our children (born or yet unborn, young or old, near or far) and our families.

Take Away for Today

1. Do you cherish your children—or your future children—as "God's best gift"?
2. Do you feel blessed to be a parent?
3. What does the psalmist mean by sweeping your enemies right off your doorstep in regard to children?

_____

_____

_____

HEAR INSTRUCTION, KNOW UNDERSTANDING

Hear, my children, the instruction of a father, and give attention to know understanding (Proverbs 4:1 NKJV).

A S children of God it is beneficial and wise to listen to our elders and pay attention to what they say so we can gain understanding. There are many things we do not know about the Kingdom and God's nature. We learn these things from reading the Word and from listening to others in whom God has placed wisdom.

Take Away for Today

1. How good are you at listening and following instructions?
2. How good are you at paying attention so you can learn?
3. How good are you at understanding what the Lord has to say to you through others?

BE EXPECTANT

*God's word: Dig ditches all over this valley. Here's what will happen—you won't hear the wind, you won't see the rain [divine advancement], but this valley is going to fill up with water [blessings] and your army and your animals will drink their fill. **This is easy for God to do;** he will also hand over Moab to you. You will ravage the country: Knock out its fortifications, level the key villages, clear-cut the orchards, clog the springs, and litter the cultivated fields with stones* (2 Kings 3:16-19).

D IVINE advancement is when God omits some stages to facilitate the fulfillment of blessing. It is natural for winds to blow and rain to fall before you enjoy water from the sky. But for the Israelites on this occasion, God said even though there would be none of these heraldic things, they will have abundance of water! You too will enjoy divine acceleration. All this means victory for you!

Take Away for Today

1. Are you expecting God to do great things for you?
2. Do you expect the best or the worst? Why?

YOUR ANOINTING
WILL BE RESTORED

As one of them was cutting down a tree, the iron axhead fell into the water. ...The man of God asked, "Where did it fall?" ...Elisha cut a stick and threw it there, and made the iron float... (2 Kings 6:5-7).

THE axhead was his means to the future, his anointing, and link to his colleagues and destiny but it fell from him! Things can fall from the best, the most honest, most careful, the most obedient person—but God is able to restore no matter what! There will be miraculous restoration of whatever is missing in your life today.

Take Away for Today

1. Has something or someone fallen from your life? Are you trusting God for restoration?

2. How can an iron axhead be made to float in water?

3. Are you ready to show God where something fell from your life so He can restore it?

LIFT UP YOUR
SPIRITUAL LEADERS IN PRAYER

Epaphras, who is one of yourselves, a servant of Christ Jesus, sends you greetings. [He is] always striving for you earnestly in his prayers, [pleading] that you may [as persons of ripe character and clear conviction] stand firm and mature [in spiritual growth], convinced and fully assured in everything willed by God (Colossians 4:12 AMP).

THE spirit of Epaphras is a valuable gift to the Body of Christ. Instead of gossiping about our leaders, when we see any perceived weakness, we should use it as an opportunity to lift up our leaders in prayer. Strive earnestly in intercession until we see spiritual maturity in our leaders. I pray today that the spirit of Epaphras will rest upon you! Pray for fresh oil from God!

Take Away for Today

1. Do you make it a regular practice to pray for your spiritual leaders?

2. Does your spiritual leader pray for you?

3. What does praying for fresh oil from God mean to you?

TREASURE INSTRUCTIONS

Dear friend, do what I tell you; treasure my careful instructions. Do what I say and you'll live well. My teaching is as precious as your eyesight—guard it! Write it out on the back of your hands; etch it on the chambers of your heart (Proverbs 7:1-3 The Message).

AGAIN the writer of Proverbs mentions instruction and how important it is in our daily lives. We are to "treasure" the Lord's instruction and do what He says so we will "live well." We are even to write what He tells us on the back of our hands and within our hearts. That is serious business! Let us be serious about learning from Him and living well.

Take Away for Today

1. If living well means learning from the Lord, are you ready to become a student?

2. Like opening a text book, are you ready to open your heart and mind to the treasures waiting to be discovered within the Bible?

STRENGTH WILL ARISE

But those who wait on the Lord shall renew their strength; they shall mount up with wings like eagles, they shall run and not be weary, they shall walk and not faint (Isaiah 40:31 NKJV).

EAGLES ride on storms to great heights! Christians should be like eagles turning adversities into victories. Like eagles wait to mount up with wings, Christians should wait upon the Lord to renew their strength. If you wait upon the Lord then it does not matter your pace; whether you are walking or running, you will not faint. As you wait upon the Lord, put your trust in God and you shall never be disappointed.

Take Away for Today

1. Has your strength been zapped by too many responsibilities, too many commitments?

2. What can you do to renew your strength?

3. Whose help do you need to run and not be weary, walk and not faint?

BLESSINGS BEYOND YOUR WILDEST DREAMS

*Bring your full tithe to the Temple treasury so there will be ample provisions in my Temple. Test me in this and see if I don't open up heaven itself to you and pour out **blessings beyond your wildest dreams**. For my part, I will defend you against marauders, protect your wheat fields and vegetable gardens against plunderers (Malachi 3:8 The Message).*

THERE is a place to experience blessings beyond your imagination, and it is also the place of responsibilities! That is why the Bible says if you are willing and obedient, you will eat the fruits of the land. Obedience has blessings, protection, and divine favor. God can bless you beyond your wildest dreams. But you have a role to play— we are told to give our full tithe to Him.

Take Away for Today

1. Are you willing to give your full tithe in exchange for "blessings beyond your wildest dreams"?

2. Do you expect God to defend you against evil if you don't offer Him your full tithe?

GODLY INFLUENCE

The good influence of godly citizens causes a city to prosper,
but the moral decay of the wicked drives it downhill (Proverbs
11:11 The Living Bible).

DURING the tumultuous political times within many countries,
it is important that godly citizens have a say in their neighbor-
hoods, cities, and their countries. Kingdom concepts and righteous
precepts are beneficial to every aspect of society. The dangerous and
radical beliefs of the few need to be balanced against the inclusive
and respectful beliefs of the many others worldwide.

Take Away for Today

1. Do your beliefs play a role in your community and
   beyond?
2. Have you witnessed the moral decay within your country?
3. Are you willing to do something to stop the decay?

INHARMONIOUS CIRCUMSTANCES

All has been heard; the end of the matter is: Fear God [revere and worship Him, knowing that He is] and keep His commandments, for this is the whole of man [the full, original purpose of his creation, the object of God's providence, the root of character, the foundation of all happiness, the adjustment to all inharmonious circumstances and conditions under the sun] and the whole [duty] for every man (Ecclesiastes 12:13 AMP).

THE present earth in the fallen state is a far cry from the harmony, peace, and joy of the original earth God created. One of the consequences of the Fall of Adam in the Garden of Eden is that disharmony entered into all aspects of humankind existence on earth. But for the redeemed of the Lord, God will adjust all inharmonious circumstances. Certain things may not fall into place right away, but rest assured the Lord God is able bring things in His perfect plan into harmony.

Take Away for Today

1. Are you living with inharmonious circumstances and conditions right now?
2. Are you resting assured that your Lord God will allow everything to fall into place at the right time?

_____

_____

_____

OUR VERY STEPS

*The very steps we take come from God; otherwise how would
we know where we're going?* (Proverbs 20:24-25 The Message)

KNOWING that each of our steps is directed by God Almighty
should bring us relief, as He is in total control and will not lead
us over a cliff or in front of a train. His path is straight and we can be
assured that as long as we stay on it, step by step we will move forward into His glorious presence.

Take Away for Today

1. Do you know where you are going?
2. Are you prepared to stay on the straight and narrow
   path that leads to your God-given destiny?

HONEST PEOPLE AND UNDERSTANDING LEADERS

*The wicked are edgy with guilt, ready to run off even when
no one's after them; honest people are relaxed and confident,
bold as lions. When the country is in chaos, everybody has a
plan to fix it—but it takes a leader of real understanding
to straighten things out* (Proverbs 28:1-2 The Message).

T HERE are many wicked people in the world edgy with guilt—
thankfully there are many more honest people who are keeping the world aligned with reason and justice. When countries are in
chaos, as is the case in many today, leaders must be put in place who
have real—godly—understanding and can set things right.

Take Away for Today

1. Are the wicked soon going to outnumber the honest
   people in your region?
2. Can you be numbered as one of the honest people—a
   leader of understanding?

LIKE THE ARMY OF GOD

*Day after day men came to help David, until he had a great
army, like the army of God* (1 Chronicles 12:22).

ANOINTING is the power of God to achieve divine purpose.
David was not yet the king and he was not in a palace, but God
anointed him and men came to him wherever he was! Anointing has
purpose, time, place, and people of maximum expression. Today may
your anointing mature to find the place, time, and people it is pur-
posed for and you will not fail. Then your family will be "like the army
of God."

Take Away for Today

1. Over the years has God brought the right people into
   your life at the right time?

2. By assisting others in their times of need, have you cultivated friends and family to respond to your requests
   for help?

_____

_____

_____

MY PRAYERS FOR YOU

In all my prayers for all of you, I always pray with joy
(Philippians 1:4).

THE prophet Isaiah says with joy you can fetch water from the well of salvation. This means you can only fully tap into the benefits of your salvation if the joy of the Lord is truly your strength in all and every circumstance. May you explore the final frontiers of Heaven upon the earth and forge ahead victoriously! May you decree a thing and it shall be established! May your mouth be sanctified as a mighty divine weapon to propel you to your destiny.

Take Away for Today

1. Will you accept these prayers of mine for you?
2. Do you believe that the prayers of believers go straight from their mouths to God's ears?

GOD WILL GATHER YOU TO FULLNESS

*"**At that time** I will gather you; **at that time** I will bring you home. I will give you honor and praise among all the peoples of the earth when I restore your fortunes before your very eyes," says the Lord (Zephaniah 3:20).*

TIME has its fullness! And every promise has its fullness in time. The passage says *"at that time"* all things will fall into the right place for you. The psalmist calls it the day of your power—*"your troops shall be willing"* (Ps. 110:3). That is the time when all those connected with your path shall align with the purpose of God in your life, friends and foes alike. This is a great promise of restoration to fullness even beyond the expectation of those affected. You are blessed and highly favored. The Lord will surely gather you to fullness!

Take Away for Today

1. When you thought your life was out of control, were you joyful when everything fell into place just at the right time?

2. Did you thank God for His presence in your life "at that time"?

_____

_____

_____

EVERY WORK OF THE SPOILER IS CANCELED

"But all who devour you will be devoured; all your enemies will go into exile. Those who plunder you will be plundered; **all who make spoil of you I will despoil.** *But I will restore you to health and heal your wounds," declares the Lord...* (Jeremiah 30:16-17).

ANY person or circumstance that spoils things when it gets to your turn is a "spoiler." Many have repetitive experience with the spoiler in their lives and it seems like a vicious circle. A spoiler spoils things whenever it gets to your turn. God promises to "despoil" every work of the spoiler in your life. This spirit must be resisted so it will flee from you. By this, I join my faith with yours and we decree that the work of the spoiler will never have dominion over your life again!

Take Away for Today

1. Has the spoiler been spoiling your plans, dreams, goals?
2. Do you allow the spoiler to infiltrate your thoughts and mind?
3. What can you do to close up the crack where the spoiler enters?

EVERY UNGODLY AND NEGATIVE ADDITION IS DISALLOWED

But He [Jesus] answered and said, "Every plant which My heavenly Father has not planted will be uprooted" (Matthew 15:13 NKJV).

THE Bible says when man was asleep, the devil planted weeds among wheat. And when the farmer saw the weeds, he exclaimed, "Didn't I plant good seeds? Where did this come from?" Evil planting is usually at the period of least alertness, the time of most vulnerability, and the time of least resistance when ungodly and negative additions sneak into people's lives. This is what Jesus declared—every negative addition to your life and circumstance is disallowed!

Take Away for Today

1. Has God had to uproot ungodliness that crept into your life while you were distracted?

2. How easy is it for you to be so focused on your everyday activities that evil seeds can be planted without your knowing?

_____

_____

_____

BE BLESSED WITH
THE PRAYER OF KING ASA

*Then Asa called to the Lord his God and said, "Lord, there is
no one like you to help the powerless against the mighty. Help
us, Lord our God, for we rely on you, and in your name we have
come against this vast army. Lord, you are our God; do not let
mere mortals prevail against you"* (2 Chronicles 14:11).

THIS was Asa's prayer at the time in his life when he was wholly
dependent on God. Those who put their trust in God will never
be disappointed. Then the Lord struck down Asa's enemies. Let this
be your prayer today, and the Lord will fight for you!

Take Away for Today

1. Do you totally rely on God and therefore render your
   enemies powerless?
2. How often do you thank God for watching over you,
   protecting you, loving you?

EVEN THOUGH

*Most of those who came from Ephraim, Manasseh, Issachar, and Zebulun had not purified themselves. But **King Hezekiah prayed for them,** and they were allowed to eat the Passover meal anyway, **even though** this was contrary to the requirements of the Law. For Hezekiah said, "May the LORD, who is good, pardon those who decide to follow the LORD, the God of their ancestors, **even though** they are not properly cleansed for the ceremony" (2 Chronicles 30:18-19 NLT).*

HEZEKIAH heard that some people were enthusiastic in serving God, but that they fell short in some regulations. Hezekiah looked beyond the weakness of mere mortals and saw the genuineness of the desire to serve God, even though their flesh failed them. He prayed for them and God forgave them and blessed them. The human flesh will fail! Even though things may seem contrary, if you stick to God—God will show Himself strong on your behalf.

Take Away for Today

1. Have you fallen short on some regulations, yet God has blessed you through His grace and mercy?

2. Even though you are not purely righteous, does God still show Himself strong on your behalf?

EVEN NOW

*"Lord," Martha said to Jesus, "if you had been here, my brother would not have died. But I know that **even now** God will give you whatever you ask"* (John 11:21-22).

A S humankind we sometimes measure God's capabilities with the limits of human ability. Humankind is limited, but God is not! Martha figured out Jesus could have saved her brother if He had come earlier, but she did not know He had the power to ask God to give Him whatever He wanted. The question is: how bad does it have to get for God not to be able to help? The truth is there is no valley too deep that God can not get you out of it. Like Martha, you may not realize that God can deliver in any circumstance. Even now I declare that God will deliver for you without fail no matter how precarious your situation may be. The God of "even now" is still able to deliver— no matter the time or the circumstance!

Take Away for Today

1. Do you think you would have had the same trust and confidence in Jesus if that was your brother who had died?

2. How would you describe the "God of even now"?

EVEN IF NOT

*Shadrach, Meshach and Abednego replied to him, "King Nebuchadnezzar, we do not need to defend ourselves before you in this matter. If we are thrown into the blazing furnace, the God we serve is able to deliver us from it, and he will deliver us from Your Majesty's hand. But **even if he does not,** we want you to know, Your Majesty, that we will not serve your gods or worship the image of gold you have set up* (Daniel 3:16-18).

THERE is difference between faith and trust in God. *"Now faith is the substance of things hoped for, the evidence of things not seen"* (Heb 11:1). So in faith, you hope for something! But trust on the other hand says regardless of the outcome, I will stick with God. They who put their trust in God will never be disappointed. The three Hebrew men trusted in the God of the Hebrews and were miraculously delivered. The heathen king shouted only the true God could save in that way!

Take Away for Today

1. How did it work out for the three who were so adamant about not betraying the Lord God? (See Daniel 3:19-25.)

2. Is your faith and trust in God as strong as this trio's confidence?

GREATNESS WILL COME

But you, Bethlehem Ephrathah, though you are small among the clans of Judah, out of you will come for me one who will be ruler over Israel, whose origins are from of old, from ancient times (Micah 5:2).

IN Micah 5:2, this was not only a prophecy about the promised Messiah, it was a prophecy about greatness emanating from something small, about excellence coming out of mediocrity, about the fact that God's ways are not our ways. Do not let anyone look down on you because of your present situation—your God will bring you into greatness.

Take Away for Today

1. Do you believe you are destined for greatness?
2. What are you doing to prepare yourself?

_____

_____

_____

THE SHEEP OF GOD'S PASTURE

He will stand and shepherd his flock in the strength of the
LORD, in the majesty of the name of the LORD his God. And
they will live securely, for then his greatness will reach to the
ends of the earth. And he will be our peace... (Micah 5:4-5).

WHEN the Lord shepherds a people, they walk in His strength; His name will be their banner and a strong tower into which they are safe and secure. His peace will not leave them and the world will see and give glory to God.

Take Away for Today

1. What comes to mind when you picture the Lord shepherding His flock of children?

2. How do you think the Lord Jesus feels when some of His flock choose to go their own way rather than follow the safe and straight path He paved for them?

3. Do you ever wander away from the peace of His shepherding?

WATCHING IN HOPE

But as for me, I watch in hope for the LORD, I wait for God my Savior; my God will hear me (Micah 7:7).

I T is a choice that you have to make every day. The challenges that want to steal your hope and future surround you everywhere you look. Your focus should not on the magnitude of the problem but on God who is able to stop you from falling and for whom nothing is too hard. It is the hope of a better tomorrow in Him that gives you zeal to face every new day.

Take Away for Today

1. Are you watching in hope for the Lord?
2. Are you waiting for God your Savior?
3. Are you speaking to Him so God will hear you?

THE SILENT WITNESSES

Listen to what the Lord says: "Stand up, plead your case before the mountains; let the hills hear what you have to say. Hear, O mountains, the Lord's accusation; listen, you everlasting foundations of the earth. For the Lord has a case against his people; he is lodging a charge against Israel" (Micah 6:1-2).

THE ground can hear, the mountain can bear witness, the earth and all its firmaments can respond to the actions and inactions of humankind and the commands of the Lord of us all. God told Cain that the ground testified against him for killing his brother instead of being his brother's keeper. Be advised—there are a host of witnesses!

Take Away for Today

1. Do you act and talk differently when you stop and realize that God is present in all your conversations and throughout every day and night?

2. Does the Lord have a case against you?

I WILL RISE AGAIN

Do not gloat over me, my enemy! Though I have fallen, I will rise. Though I sit in darkness, the Lord will be my light (Micah 7:8).

DO not write off a person—do not gloat over someone, even an enemy. God changes times and seasons, and He brings one up and brings another down. So do not even gloat over your enemy's misfortune because God can turn things around in seconds.

Take Away for Today

1. Other than the "evil one" who wants to destroy you because you are a child of God, do you have other "enemies"? What makes them so?

2. Are there those whom you have written off as enemies, losers? What do you think God's feelings are about such actions?

FROM DARKNESS TO LIGHT

...He will bring me out into the light; I will see his righteousness. Then my enemy will see it and will be covered with shame; she who said to me, "Where is the Lord your God?" My eyes will see her downfall; even now she will be trampled underfoot like mire in the streets (Micah 7:9-10).

YOUR eyes will see the downfall of those who say, "Where is your God?" Those who challenge the God in you will surely face the wrath of His anger. Shame and despair will fall on those who despise the name of our God.

Take Away for Today

1. Have others scoffed at you for believing in God?
2. How do you respond to scoffers?
3. Do you have faith that God is the ultimate revenger?

_____

_____

_____

HIS MOMENTARY ANGER

*Who is a God like you, who pardons sin and forgives the
transgression of the remnant of his inheritance? You do not stay
angry forever but delight to show mercy. You will again have
compassion on us; you will tread our sins underfoot and hurl
all our iniquities into the depths of the sea* (Micah 7:18-19).

GOD is a merciful God, and He forgives all our sins and iniquities. His anger is only for a moment. If we confess our sins
and humble ourselves in the hands of the Almighty, He will bless us.
The book of Zephaniah admonishes to seek righteousness and see
humility, and the Lord will visit and bless us: *"Seek the LORD, all you
humble of the land, you who do what he commands. Seek righteousness, seek humility; perhaps you will be sheltered on the day of the
LORD's anger"* (Zephaniah 2:3).

Take Away for Today

1. Are you thankful that the Lord's anger is but a moment?
2. How long do you stay angry? Do you hold grudges that
   last for days, years?
3. Are you seeking righteousness and humility as the Bible
   suggests?

THE LORD REJOICES OVER YOU

The Lord your God is with you, the Mighty Warrior who saves. He will take great delight in you; in his love he will no longer rebuke you, he will rejoice over you with singing (Zephaniah 3:17).

THE Lord will rejoice over you with singing. You were made for His pleasure. So when the Lord rejoices over you, you must certainly be fulfilling your divine purpose.

Of course we are to rejoice and delight in our Lord as well. As Isaiah 61:10 says, *"I delight greatly in the Lord; my soul rejoices in my God. For he has clothed me with garments of salvation and arrayed me in a robe of his righteousness, as a bridegroom adorns his head like a priest, and as a bride adorns herself with her jewels."* May the delight and rejoicing be reciprocal—eternally.

Take Away for Today

1. Have there been times when you felt the Lord rejoicing over you with singing?
2. Does knowing God delights in you give you hope and a joyful heart?
3. Have you delighted greatly in the Lord lately?

WORK AND PLAY

Work your garden—you'll end up with plenty of food; play and party—you'll end up with an empty plate. Committed and persistent work pays off; get-rich-quick schemes are ripoffs (Proverbs 28:19-20 The Message).

HARD work is still the best way of providing for your family. God structured the world in a way that workers reap what they sow, as do those who don't work. There seems to be a prevailing attitude worldwide that people need not work to receive benefits. The Bible says we should provide for the poor but everyone who can work should work, the reward of a good work is bountiful.

Take Away for Today

1. Are you a hard-worker who appreciates earning what you deserve to receive?
2. Have you witnessed those who would rather receive a government hand-out rather than work for a living?
3. Where does this type of economic system lead?

_____

_____

_____

A GREAT MODEL OF PRAYER

Now, Lord my God, you have made your servant king in place of my father David. But I am only a little child and do not know how to carry out my duties. Your servant is here among the people you have chosen, a great people, too numerous to count or number. So give your servant a discerning heart to govern your people and to distinguish between right and wrong. For who is able to govern this great people of yours?
(1 Kings 3:7-9).

THIS prayer of King Solomon reveals true selflessness, meekness, desire for righteousness, desire for service and justice. God was moved, and King Solomon was blessed beyond his expectation. It is always best to come before God with a humble and contrite heart.

Take Away for Today

1. What are five important aspects of this prayer?

2. Make this prayer personal. For example, "Now, Lord my God, You have made me, Your servant, in place of my parents...give Your servant a discerning heart to help me shepherd my family and to distinguish between right and wrong...

THE MOTHERHOOD TEST

Then the king said, "Bring me a sword." So they brought a sword for the king. He then gave an order: "Cut the living child in two and give half to one and half to the other." The woman whose son was alive was filled with compassion for her son and said to the king, "Please, my lord, give her the living baby! Don't kill him!" But the other said, "Neither I nor you shall have him. Cut him in two!" Then the king gave his ruling: "Give the living baby to the first woman. Do not kill him; she is his mother" (1 Kings 3:24-27).

THE true test of divine wisdom and motherhood is respect for human life! The woman who opted to preserve the baby's life is the true mother of the baby. In the world today, there are many who have given birth to children biologically, but if they don't have respect for the lives of the children, they are not mothers! As mothers, please stop and think of the lives of your children; pause, reflect, and respect the lives of your children over your earthly ambitions, corporate ladder climbing, and the satisfaction of personal gratifications. Tomorrow will surely come and the dust will definitely settle, then what will be said!

Take Away for Today

1. How respectful are you of human life? Do you condone abortion? Capital punishment?
2. Does your culture and society respect human life? Give examples to support your answer.

_____

_____

TRUE WISDOM SPEAKS FOR ITSELF

When all Israel heard the verdict the king had given, they held the king in awe, because they saw that he had wisdom from God to administer justice (1 Kings 3:28).

WISDOM has a voice! It speaks every day for those who deserve to have her. Sometimes divine wisdom can be so loud that everyone will have no choice but acknowledge her. Other times divine wisdom comes as a whisper, nudging us on and in the right direction.

Take Away for Today

1. How wise are you? Do you garner your wisdom from text books, others, or God?
2. Do you seek God for His wisdom before making decisions?

PRAYERS FOR A VICTORIOUS DAY

I encourage you to read the following Scriptures and then focus on the prompts to have a joyous and victorious day in the Lord!

- Psalm 32:5 – acknowledge your sins
- Daniel 9:17-19 – ask God, give ear and hear, open His eyes and see
- Psalm 18:17 – ask God to rescue you from powerful enemies
- Psalm 30:11 – ask God to turns your wailing to dancing
- Psalm 31:15 – acknowledge your times are in His hands
- Psalm 20:6-8 – put your trust is in God who saves His anointed
- Isaiah 8:10 – ask God to frustrate the plans of the enemy

Take Away for Today

1. Which one of the Scriptures made you contemplate the most? The least?

2. Which one of the Scriptures brought you the most peace of heart?

BREAK THE SPIRIT OF STAGNATION

TO break the spirit of stagnation and move forward in your spiritual and daily walk, pray and meditate on these prayers:

- God decrees on your behalf: *"I am going to put an end to this proverb"* (the saying, good promises not fulfilled). *"None of My words will be delayed any longer"* (see Ezek. 12:22,28). No more delay!

- Declare *"You have stayed long enough...break camp and advance"* (Deut. 1:6-7). It is time to advance!

- Proclaim that this is your divine overtaking season: *"Then the Lord gave special strength to Elijah...he...ran ahead [overtook] of Ahab's chariot all the way to the entrance of Jezreel"* (1 Kings 18:46 NLT). It is time for divine acceleration.

Pursue, overtake, and recover all!

Take Away for Today

1. If you are not advancing or making progress, you are stagnant. Have you a feeling of stagnation?

2. Have you been making marked progress in your spiritual walk? Your marriage? Your career? Your relationships?

_____

_____

_____

GOD HAS THE LAST WORD

*Mortals make elaborate plans, but **God has the last word.** Humans are satisfied with whatever looks good; God probes for what is good. Put God in charge of your work, then what you've planned will take place. God made everything with a place and purpose; even the wicked are included—but for judgment* (Proverbs 16:1-4 The Message).

THROUGHOUT this year of devotions, there has been a theme of focusing on God and getting closer to Him in every way, every day. We would be remiss if we didn't include how important God is in our workplace and in the world of economics and politics. As the passage from Proverbs says, "Mortals make elaborate plans, but God has the last word." This is so very true—as He probes for what is good, not like worldly leaders who are satisfied with whatever looks good.

Take Away for Today

1. Do you go to God for the last word?
2. Do you trust in Him and His Word rather than world leaders who many times have their own agendas that do not align with God's will?

THE GLORY RETURNS TO THE TEMPLE

Then the man brought me to the gate facing east, and I saw the glory of the God of Israel coming from the east. His voice was like the roar of rushing waters and the land was radiant with his glory. The glory of the Lord entered the temple..."
(Ezekiel 43:1-2,4).

REMEMBER, you are the temple of God! May the glory of God cover you wherever you go and make you radiant! As people come in contact with you throughout the day and weeks to come, may they sense a peace and wisdom about you that they want to get close to—then point them to the Source of your peace and wisdom.

Take Away for Today

1. How would you define the "glory of God"?
2. Have you witnessed the land "radiant with His glory"?

LET US PRESS ON

Let us acknowledge the Lord; let us press on to acknowledge him. As surely as the sun rises, he will appear; he will come to us like the winter rains, like the spring rains that water the earth (Hosea 6:3).

THE Bible says in Daniel 11:32 (NKJV) that "the people who know their God shall be strong, and carry out great exploits." To know Him is one of the reasons we should press on until we attain revelatory knowledge of Him so we can do exploits and bring glory to His Kingdom.

Take Away for Today

1. Are you committed to "press on" throughout this New Year—acknowledging Him for all the good things in your world?

2. What "great exploits" do you want to accomplish for His glory this year?

GOD HAS THE FINAL SAY

*Moderation is better than muscle, self-control better than political power. Make your motions and cast your votes, but **God has the final say*** (Proverbs 16:32-33).

I T behoves us to be slow to anger, for losing our tempers and making rash decisions is not the way of God. When Jesus was presented with a woman who was caught in adultery and people were screaming and taunting and demanding a response from Him, rather than getting caught up in the rage of the moment, he stooped and calmly wrote something in the dirt. We must exercise self-control and voice our calm and rational opinions in the midst of every situation—righteous people need to be heard above all the fracas.

Take Away for Today

1. Do you consider yourself a moderate, self-controlled person?

2. Is being involved in the political process a priority in your life?

MAKE YOUR MINISTRY FULL PROOF

But you be watchful in all things, endure afflictions, do the work of an evangelist, fulfill your ministry (2 Timothy 4:5 NKJV).

I F you are a believer, you have a ministry. Everyone has a ministry! Fulfilling this ministry is crucially essential to your life and the life of God's Kingdom. This is all that counts! That was the prayer of Paul for Timothy and is my prayer for you today.

I pray also "that you may [as persons of ripe character and clear conviction] stand firm and mature [in spiritual growth], convinced and fully assured in everything willed by God" (Col. 4:12 AMP).

Take Away for Today

1. How successful have you been at fulfilling your ministry?
2. What can you do to improve your role as an evangelist?

GOD IS FAITHFUL TO FULFILL HIS PROMISES

You have kept what You promised Your servant David my father; You have both spoken with Your mouth and fulfilled it with Your hand, as it is this day (2 Chronicles 6:15 NKJV).

RECOGNIZING God's faithfulness to His promises, King Solomon says in his prayer of dedication for the temple that He kept His promises. Centuries later, the apostle Paul said that all of God's promises are "yes" in Christ (see 2 Cor. 1:20). May this be true for your life also! Pray today and have faith in God that He will fulfill all His good promises concerning you.

Take Away for Today

1. Are you faithful to fulfill all of the promises you make? To God? To your family? To your co-workers?

2. If you are unable to keep a promise, are you quick to acknowledge your slight and to make it right?

THEIR SOULS WERE KNIT TOGETHER

Jonathan said to David, "Go in peace, for we have sworn friendship with each other in the name of the Lord...
(1 Samuel 20:42).

B ECAUSE of their deep friendship, Jonathan *"was grieved for David at his father's shameful treatment of David"* (1 Sam. 20:34). He warned him of his father's plan and told him he should leave. David recognized what a good friend he had in Jonathan. The Bible says they wept together, "but David more so" (v. 41). Their souls were "knit" together.

Take Away for Today

1. Friends are gifts from God—do you value your friends?
2. What have you done lately to reach out to others who may need a friend?

THE FATE OF A FALSE PROPHET

Then the prophet Jeremiah said to Hananiah the prophet, "Listen, Hananiah! The Lord has not sent you, yet you have persuaded this nation to trust in lies. Therefore, this is what the Lord says: 'I am about to remove you from the face of the earth. This very year you are going to die, because you have preached rebellion against the Lord.'" In the seventh month of that same year, Hananiah the prophet died (Jeremiah 28:15-17).

FALSE prophecy draws people away from God and draws people's attention to the false prophet. False prophecy is often motivated by self-exaltation and material gains. There is no big or small false prophecy, one is as dangerous as the other; avoid it and all its ramifications. God killed the false prophet Hananiah.

Take Away for Today

1. Have you encountered a false prophet? What was your reaction?

2. Can you name infamous false prophets who gained local, regional, or national recognition before they were exposed?

DIVINE MANDATE TO INCREASE

Build houses and settle down; plant gardens and eat what they produce. Marry and have sons and daughters; find wives for your sons and give your daughters in marriage, so that they too may have sons and daughters. Increase in number there; do not decrease. Also, seek the peace and prosperity of the city to which I have carried you into exile. Pray to the Lord for it, because if it prospers, you too will prosper (Jeremiah 29:5-7).

GOD moves people around, and it does not matter how you got to where you are. Know for sure that God watches over all things! Why you are living where you are? Only God knows—you are in that place for such time as this! With the realization will come divine mandate to increase—and prosper.

Take Away for Today

1. Are you seeking peace and prosperity for the place where you live?

2. Do you believe that God planted you where you are so you could make an eternal difference in the lives of people around you?

3. Are you ready to settle down and produce and prosper?

SEEK GOD, FIND GOD

"Then you will call upon me and come and pray to me, and I will listen to you. You will seek me and find me when you seek me with all your heart. I will be found by you," declares the Lord... (Jeremiah 29:12-14).

WHEN you seek God, you will find Him. When you call upon Him, He will answer. When you pray to Him, He will listen. When you open your heart to Him, He will fill it to overflowing with His mercy, grace, and love for you. "When you call on Me, when you come and pray to Me, I'll listen." The Message version of the Bible says it this way, *"When you come looking for me, you'll find me. Yes, when you get serious about finding me and want it more than anything else, I'll make sure you won't be disappointed."*

Take Away for Today

1. Are you comforted by the fact, the truth, the promise that the Lord will listen to you when you call on Him?

2. Are you trusting in His promise that when you seek Him with all your heart, you will find Him?

THE EVIL ONES NEVER LEARN

Will those who do evil never learn? They eat up my people like bread and wouldn't think of praying to the Lord. Terror will grip them, for God is with those who obey him. The wicked frustrate the plans of the oppressed, but the Lord will protect his people. Who will come from Mount Zion to rescue Israel? When the Lord restores his people, Jacob will shout with joy, and Israel will rejoice (Psalm 14:4-7 NLT).

DAVID writes that those who do evil will never learn—that they eat up the people like bread and don't pray. Terror grips these people and they torment the oppressed. But! God protects the people who obey Him and pray. He will restore us unto Himself whenever we seek Him. Let us always be on God's side—learning, obeying, and praying.

Take Away for Today

1. Are you a life-long learner?
2. Do you believe that there is always something more to learn?

WE WILL NOT DECREASE

From them will come songs of thanksgiving and the sound of rejoicing. I will add to their numbers, and they will not be decreased; I will bring them honor, and they will not be disdained (Jeremiah 30:19).

B ETWEEN increase and decrease there are two other dimensions—1) stagnation when there is no increase and no decrease and 2) when increase is balanced by decrease and there is no progress! But notice in the Scripture verse above that God will add to your number (true increase) and you will not decrease (retrogression). You will experience true progress.

Take Away for Today

1. Have there been times in your life when you felt stagnated? There was no advancement in any area of your life?

2. Have there been times in your life when you felt that the status quo would be your lot in life—there would be no change?

3. What did you do to climb out of those times and move forward and upward?

_____

_____

_____

Reading the Bible in a Year: Joshua 4-6 and Luke 2:1-24.

MEDITATE ON THIS

"You, Lord, keep my lamp burning; my God turns my darkness into light. ...It is God who arms me with strength and keeps my way secure. He makes my feet like the feet of a deer; He causes [enables] me to stand on the heights. He trains my hands for battle; my arms can bend a bow of bronze. You make your saving help my shield, and your right hand sustains me; your help has made me great" (Psalm 18:28-35).

STAND on the heights—let this be a reality in your life. One way this can happen is to come to the realization that when you spend time on God and with God, you make room for God and His power. Always remember this! May this be your testimony.

Take Away for Today

1. When you feel gloomy and darkness seems to surround you, how long does it take you to realize that God is more than able to turn your darkness into light and constantly keeps His lamp burning brightly around you?

2. Do you daily arm yourself with God's shield and take hold of His right hand which will sustain you through any and all circumstances?

BITING THE HANDS
THAT FEED YOU

How much more severely do you think someone deserves to be punished who has trampled the Son of God underfoot, who has treated as an unholy thing the blood of the covenant that sanctified them, and who has insulted the Spirit of grace?
(Hebrews 10:29)

AFTER reading this verse in Hebrews, I believe it comes down to biting the hands that feed you! Whenever we trample on the grace of God by which we were redeemed, we insult the Son of God; and if we fail to treat others as He has treated us, we are biting the finger of Christ!

Take Away for Today

1. Are you guilty of biting the hands that feed you?
2. Could you be charged with biting the finger of Christ?

A SEASON OF RECOMPENSE

They will not labor in vain, nor will they bear children doomed to misfortune; for they will be a people blessed by the Lord, they and their descendants with them (Isaiah 65:23).

YOU have come to a season of recompense of rewards. As the Bible says your labor of love will not go in vain; your goodness and righteousness will speak for you. There was a time in Jacob's life when he came to this season (see Gen. 30:33). The Lord will remember you and break any limitation around you (see Gen. 8:1). The dews of heaven will come upon you (see Zech. 8:12). To the blind man this was the season that Jesus said to him, *"Do you believe that I am able to do this?"* (Matt. 9:28).

Take Away for Today

1. Do you accept this prophecy that you are entering into a season or recompense of rewards? Why or why not?

2. Do you believe that Jesus is able to do this for you?

THE FRUITS OF GOD'S FAVOR

This is what the Lord says: "In the time of my favor I will answer you, and in the day of salvation I will help you; I will keep you and will make you to be a covenant for the people, to restore the land and to reassign its desolate inheritances." But this is what the Lord says: "Yes, captives will be taken from warriors, and plunder retrieved from the fierce; I will contend with those who contend with you, and your children I will save" (Isaiah 49:8,25).

FAVOR has fruits and they manifest as divine enablement. The following are some of the ways favor will reveal itself in your life. God will:

- *Answer* you
- *Help* you
- *Keep* you
- *Make* a covenant with you
- *Restore* the land
- *Reassign* its desolate inheritance
- *Contend* with your enemies
- *Save* your children

Take Away for Today

1. Is there anything better than reaping the harvest of God's fruit?

2. Is there any higher reward than receiving and eating fruit from God the Father, the Creator?

BEWARE OF STRANGE DOCTRINE

*Do not be carried away by all kinds of **strange teachings.***
It is good for our hearts to be strengthened by grace, not by
ceremonial foods, which are of no value to those who do so
(Hebrews 13:9).

T HE King James Version states this verse this way: "Be not carried about with divers and strange doctrines. For it is a good thing that the heart be established with grace; not with meats, which have not profited them that have been occupied therein" (Hebrews 13:9). Strange teachings or doctrines are often melodramatic philosophy or dramatic manifestations that are contrary to the teachings of God. Often they may be attention seeking but are in reality empty and bear no tangible relevance to the essence of godly life. Keep your mind and thoughts on Jesus Christ and Him crucified! He is the author and finisher of our faith.

Take Away for Today

1. Has someone tempted you to learn strange teachings?
2. Do you have friends or family who have followed after strange teachings?
3. What is the best and only way to determine if teachings or doctrine are godly or evil?

THE FATE OF THE WICKED

What are worthless and wicked people like? They are constant liars, signaling their deceit with a wink of the eye, a nudge of the foot, or the wiggle of fingers. Their perverted hearts plot evil, and they constantly stir up trouble. But they will be destroyed suddenly, broken in an instant beyond all hope of healing (Proverbs 6:12-15 NLT).

NEVER envy the wicked; their reign, if any, is always short-lived! The wicked are on a slippery slope, and unless they repent will surely be destroyed. That is why the Bible says they will be suddenly destroyed and have no hope of healing. Goodness will never fail. Do something good, and in due season it will speak out for you.

Take Away for Today

1. Have you ever considered this description of a wicked person?
2. Do you think that modern-day culture promotes and/or condones this type of behavior?

GOD CALLS AND PROTECTS

"Get yourself ready! Stand up and say to them whatever I command you. Do not be terrified by them.... Today I have made you a fortified city, an iron pillar and a bronze wall to stand against the whole land.... They will fight against you but will not overcome you, for I am with you and I will rescue you," declares the Lord (Jeremiah 1:17-19).

WHEN God calls, He also protects. This is also your portion! You need not be afraid to step out into your calling because God will equip you, protect you, and give you the courage you need to make good things happen. Today, trust and obey, and know that He will protect you and guide your steps!

Take Away for Today

1. Has God called you but you are afraid to step out for fear of evil overwhelming you as you serve the Lord?

2. Is it time you "Get yourself ready" and stand up and say what the Lord commands you to say?

THE FUTURE OF
A GOOD PERSON

*Blessed is the one who does not walk in step with the wicked
or stand in the way that sinners take or sit in the
company of mockers* (Psalm 1:1).

THE future of good people is bright! *"The good man walks along
in the ever-brightening light of God's favor; the dawn gives way to
morning splendor, while the evil man gropes and stumbles in the dark"*
(Prov. 4:18-19 The Living Bible). So today, let your light so shine that
people will glorify your God. *"Not so the wicked! They are like chaff
that the wind blows away. Therefore the wicked will not stand in the
judgment, nor sinners in the assembly of the righteous. For the LORD
watches over the way of the righteous, but the way of the wicked leads
to destruction"* (Ps. 1:4-6).

Take Away for Today

1. How careful are you to not walk with the wicked or keep
   company with sinners and mockers?

2. How bright is your light shining so that the wicked, sinners, and mockers will want to know the Source of your
   light?

Reading the Bible in a Year: Joshua 23-24 and Luke 6:27-49.

AS A PARENT CARRIES A CHILD

Do not be terrified; do not be afraid of them. The Lord your God, who is going before you, will fight for you, as he did for you in Egypt, before your very eyes, and in the wilderness. There you saw how the Lord your God carried you, as a father carries his son, all the way you went until you reached this place (Deuteronomy 1:29-31).

HOW reassuring it is to realize that God carries you as a natural parent carries a child—with tenderness and ultimate affection. And it does not matter whether you are young or old. It does not matter to God; He is the Father of all. Today don't be afraid, He will be with you and fight your battles. On the contrary, Moses warned the Israelites saying, *"But the LORD said to me, 'Tell them, "Do not go up and fight, because I will not be with you. You will be defeated by your enemies"'"* (Deut. 1:42). In other words, you cannot fight and win on your own strength because it is God who gives power for victory.

Take Away for Today

1. Before you go into "battle" at home, church, or at work, do you stop first and ask God if He is going with you?

2. How many battles do you think you would win if you first asked God if He is on your side?

A LAMPSTAND OF GOD

This is how the lampstand was made: It was made of hammered gold—from its base to its blossoms. The lampstand was made exactly like the pattern the Lord had shown Moses (Numbers 8:4).

YOU are a lampstand of God on earth! May your light never go off; may the Lord keep your light burning, and may your oil never cease flowing! *"They made the lampstand of pure gold* [meaning there is divine substance in you]. *They hammered out* [meaning all your past experiences have molded you and made you who you are today] *its base and shaft, and made its flowerlike cups, buds and blossoms of one piece* [meaning you are now standing firm, whole and in unity with the Spirit after it all] *with them"* (Exod. 37:17).

Take Away for Today

1. Are you functioning as a lampstand in your home, your workplace, your church?

2. Does your lampstand turn dark? What have you done to make it stop shining, and what do you do to regain the light?

THIS WORD IS FOR YOU

No one will be able to stand up against you all the days of your life. As I was with Moses, so I will be with you; I will never leave you nor forsake you. Be strong and courageous...
(Joshua 1:5-6).

THESE were the words of God to Joshua at a critical moment of transition in his life. I believe this is what God is saying to you right now! Like Joshua, often we feel the challenges in our lives are impossible, but if God says He is with you, no one can be against you. Your season has come because you now have double advantage; He is with you and promises that no one can stand up against you. Be bold and indeed be courageous!

Take Away for Today

1. Knowing what God said to Joshua and what God did for Moses, can you rest assured that He will do the same for you?

2. Is there any problem that God cannot handle?

LOOK AND LIVE

The Lord said to Moses, "Make a snake and put it up on a pole; anyone who is bitten can look at it and live." So Moses made a bronze snake and put it up on a pole. Then when anyone was bitten by a snake and looked at the bronze snake, they lived (Numbers 21:8-9).

WHEN the Israelites were in the wilderness, when people were bitten by a poisonous snake and looked up to the bronze snake hung on the pole, they lived and did not die. This was a symbol of the pre-incarnate Jesus Christ. This Old Testament occurrence was a symbol of what was to come! So now, whoever looks up to Jesus will be delivered from every predicament.

Take Away for Today

1. How often do you look up to Jesus so you can live through your trials and troubles?

2. With all the poisonous, worldly situations and sins surrounding you today, will you take the time to look up to your Savior hanging on the cross?

Reading the Bible in a Year: Judges 8-9 and Luke 8:22-56.

THE SPIRIT OF GRACE

You have not come to a mountain that can be touched and that is burning with fire; to darkness, gloom and storm; to a trumpet blast or to such a voice speaking words that those who heard it begged that no further word be spoken to them, because they could not bear what was commanded: If even an animal touches the mountain, it must be stoned. The sight was so terrifying that Moses said, I am trembling with fear. But you have come...to Jesus the mediator of a new covenant, and to the sprinkled blood that speaks a better word than the blood of Abel (Hebrews 12:18-24).

IN this age of dispensation, grace and mercy always triumphs over judgment. In the era of Moses or the law, people were punished for disobeying the laws, but now Jesus paid the full price for us! We are free indeed—not to continue in sin and lawlessness, but in the freedom of inputted righteousness now and forever.

Take Away for Today

1. What do you think it would have been like living under an oppressive set of laws?

2. How grateful are you to be living under God's generous grace and mercy?

3. Because of the shed blood of Jesus, you can live free from terror. Have you thanked Him today?

MERCY TRIUMPHS
OVER JUDGMENT

Speak and act as those who are going to be judged by the law that gives freedom, because judgment without mercy will be shown to anyone who has not been merciful. Mercy triumphs over judgment (James 2:12-13).

I F we live in the dispensation of grace, we should not only receive mercy but be prepared to grant others' mercy or forgiveness— even when we have been hurt. The Bible says forgive us our trespasses as we forgive those who trespass against us. Forgiveness is essential for living a spiritually, physically, mentally, and emotionally healthy life.

Take Away for Today

1. Grace and mercy works both ways—we receive from God and we should give to others. Is this how you believe and live?

2. How merciful are you on a scale from 1 to 10? What can you do to improve that score?

3. Are you willing to be forgiving in exchange for being totally healthy?

GOD WILL PROTECT AND PROPEL YOU TO DESTINY

And Manoah said to his wife, "We shall surely die, because we have seen God!" But his wife said to him, "If the LORD had desired to kill us, He would not have accepted a burnt offering and a grain offering from our hands, nor would He have shown us all these things, nor would He have told us such things as these at this time" (Judges 13:22-23 NKJV).

THE promises of God are protective; His shield embodies protection, propelling power and preserving force. His promises are His prophetic utterances and since His word or prophetic promises will not return to Him void, they keep you against all odds until they are fulfilled. Do you have a promise yet unfilled? Like Manoah's wife said, let me say to you, you will not die before they are fulfilled! He has not brought you this far to abandon you or let you down! Your best days are ahead of you.

Take Away for Today

1. Wow! Does knowing that your best days are ahead of you make you want to jump for joy?

2. Are you looking forward to fulfilling your God-given destiny?

THE WISE AND THE KNOW-IT-ALLS

*The wise accumulate knowledge—a true treasure; know-it-alls
talk too much—a sheer waste* (Proverbs 10:14 The Message).

WE have all encountered wise people who are blessings to their
friends, co-workers, church leaders, and all they meet. We have
also all encountered know-it-alls who brag and act arrogantly. The difference between the two groups of people is immense. Let us strive to
be wise and become true treasures to all who come to know us.

Take Away for Today

1. How do you feel when you are around someone who is
   truly wise?
2. How do you feel when you are around a know-it-all?
3. Which one are you the majority of the time?

_____

_____

_____

FAITH IS MADE COMPLETE BY YOUR ACTIONS

You see that his faith and his actions were working together, and his faith was made complete by what he did (James 2:22).

FAITH without work (action) is dead. If you have faith today in something, prove it by the work you do with it. Many profess faith yet do not put faith into action. When people see faithful people helping others, it shows them God's Kingdom in action, it gives them a reality of faith. James also tells us, *"If one of you says to them, 'Go in peace; keep warm and well fed,' but does nothing about their physical needs, what good is it? In the same way, faith by itself, if it is not accompanied by action, is dead. But someone will say, 'You have faith; I have deeds.' Show me your faith without deeds, and I will show you my faith by my deeds"* (James 2:16-18).

Take Away for Today

1. Did some "work" come to mind when you read James 2:22?

2. What work has God called you to do for Him today?

THE LORD REMEMBERS

But God remembered Noah and all the wild animals and the livestock that were with him in the ark, and he sent a wind over the earth, and the waters receded (Genesis 8:1).

GOD never forgets! Our acts of obedience and adherence to His principles activate our dormant promises and then God puts the promises into action. When your longstanding promises are put into motion, it is equivalent to God's remembrance. We are blessed with all blessings in heavenly places, but God actualizes those promises in our lives when He activates them. *"Early the next morning they arose and worshiped before the LORD and then went back to their home at Ramah. Elkanah made love to his wife Hannah, and **the LORD remembered her"*** (1 Sam. 1:19).

Take Away for Today

1. Acts of obedience activate dormant promises—have you missed blessings by acts of disobedience?

2. Do you adhere to God's principles so He can put His promises into action?

DO NOT ABUSE HIS GRACE

If we deliberately keep on sinning after we have received the knowledge of the truth, no sacrifice for sins is left (Hebrews 10:26).

TO know Jesus' sacrifice and ignore Him is to abuse His grace. Sin has a gripping effect, and its pleasure can be enticing. Willful sins—premeditated actions the sinner knows is wrong yet commits them anyway for the pleasure of the sin—God says are abominations.

Take Away for Today

1. Are you committing willful sins?
2. After reading Hebrews 10:26 do you now realize the seriousness of premeditated sin?

_____

_____

_____

BEFORE YOUR VERY EYES

Has any god ever tried to take for himself one nation out of another nation, by testings, by signs and wonders, by war, by a mighty hand and an outstretched arm, or by great and awesome deeds, like all the things the LORD your God did for you in Egypt before your very eyes? (Deuteronomy 4:34).

GOD indeed showed Himself strong on behalf of the Israelites when He took them out of Egypt. In this verse we see the various ways God can show Himself strong on your behalf: by testings (allowing you to go through some things) God can show His strength; by miraculous signs and wonders, God can show supremacy on your behalf; by war, demonstration of His mighty hands; and through awesome deeds, God can reveal His strength on your behalf!

Take Away for Today

1. Has God shown Himself strong on your behalf?
2. Has God done amazing things right before your very eyes?

_____

_____

_____

HIS BOUNDLESS BLESSINGS

He will love you and bless you and increase your numbers. He will bless the fruit of your womb, the crops of your land—your grain, new wine and oil—the calves of your herds and the lambs of your flocks in the land that he swore to your forefathers to give you. You will be blessed more than any other people; none of your men or women will be childless, nor will any of your livestock be without young (Deuteronomy 7:13-14).

THE Bible also says that the blessings of God make you rich and add no sorrow. Notice the promises in this passage from Deuteronomy 7; blessings all round, everywhere you may turn, blessings await you. See the allegory here: *increase in number* refers to expansion and acquisition; *the fruit of your womb* refers to your posterity and the generation after you; *the crops of your land* is the work of your hands and your inheritance, and *the calves of your herd* refers to the management of your wealth.

Take Away for Today

1. Are you prepared to receive all the blessings that the Lord intends for you?

2. In what specific ways do you think the Lord wants to bless you personally?

Reading the Bible in a Year: 1 Samuel 7-9 and Luke 13:1-21.

THE ENVIRONMENT COUNTS

Do not bring a detestable thing into your house or you, like it, will be set apart for destruction. Regard it as vile and utterly detest it, for it is set apart for destruction (Deuteronomy 7:26).

B E mindful of the things you allowed into your midst. Things dedicated to idols can be point of contact for the devil and his agents to gain access into your household. Evil spirits are territorial spirits! They try to claim places and their environment. The Bible says contamination with accursed things can lead to eventual destruction. Examine carefully when buying second-hand or used items; and whenever you get a used thing, it is a wise move to pray over it and rededicate it to the Lord.

Take Away for Today

1. Have you had to pray over something that you considered vile and detestable?

2. What type of things do you think may be contaminated or could lead to destruction if you allowed them into your home or workplace?

THE LORD CREATES WEALTH

But remember the Lord your God, for it is he who gives you the ability to produce wealth... (Deuteronomy 8:18).

WE so often forget that it is the Lord who gives us the ability to produce wealth. In Him we live, move, and have our being! When you are rich, remember there are many others with similar ideas and potentials, but never had the chance of putting the ideas into practice. If you are poor, remember also God can make you rich in a split second. By your own strength, you will not prevail, so put your confidence in God because every good thing comes from Him.

Take Away for Today

1. Do you consider yourself rich or poor financially? Spiritually?

2. Have you asked the Lord to give you the ability to produce wealth? (It is not a selfish request if you then use your wealth to help others.)

_____

_____

_____

GREAT CHALLENGES
BRING GREAT TESTIMONIES

...You know about them and have heard it said: "Who can stand up against the Anakites?" But be assured today that the Lord your God is the one who goes across ahead of you like a devouring fire. He will destroy them; he will subdue them before you. And you will drive them out and annihilate them quickly, as the Lord has promised you (Deuteronomy 9:2-3).

IF God is with you, remember, it will turn out for testimony no matter the challenge that may confront you now. God will take the glory out of it, and He will go ahead of you in every situation like a devouring fire consuming every daunting challenge along the way! May you be comforted today and every day knowing that the Lord is going before you—into the workplace, the school, the home full of turmoil. Lean on Him.

Take Away for Today

1. Do you know pessimistic people who always look for the worst in every situation?

2. Are you an optimistic person who can see God in every situation and know He has promised to go ahead of you, paving the way with mercy and victory?

THE FRUIT OF THE LIGHT

*For you were once darkness, but now **you are light in the Lord**.*
Live as children of light (for the fruit of the light [Spirit] consists
in all goodness, righteousness and truth) (Ephesians 5:8-9).

GOD is the Father of Light. You are light in the midst of gross darkness on earth. So let your Light so shine that the world will honor your Father! As light, let goodness, righteousness, and truth radiate from you because these are the fruit of light! The world is hungry for the fruit of light—give those around you eternal nourishment by sharing the Word with them.

Take Away for Today

1. Are you living as a child of the light?
2. Does your presence bring light into the dark corners of the world?

IF YOU BELIEVE,
YOU CAN HAVE IT

And without faith it is impossible to please God, because anyone who comes to him must believe that he exists and that he rewards those who earnestly seek him (Hebrews 11:6).

OFTEN we may not have much to show for the commitment to the things of God, but we are assured of this: our God rewards those who seek Him. Because you know God exists and that rewards are awaiting you, why not share that Good News with your co-workers and people you stand in line with at the grocery store. You will definitely leave an impression.

Take Away for Today

1. Why do you think that "without faith it is impossible to please God"?

2. Why does He reward believers who seek Him?

_____

_____

_____

LOOKING AHEAD

*For he was looking forward to the city with foundations, whose architect and builder is God. He regarded disgrace for the sake of Christ as of greater value than the treasures of Egypt, because he was **looking ahead to his reward.** By faith he left Egypt, not fearing the king's anger; he persevered because he saw him who is invisible* (Hebrews 11:10,26-27).

I T is better to suffer on the side of righteousness than to run after the joy of the momentary pleasure of wilderness. Disgrace for the sake of Christ is more valuable than anything the world has to offer. Today, do not be moved by what you see with your physical eyes; rather, look up and see Him who is invisible and He will surely reward you.

Take Away for Today

1. Do you focus more on what is in front of you or what is ahead?

2. Do you believe that you can see the invisible?

_____

_____

_____

FAITH REVEALS REALITY

By faith we understand that the universe was formed at God's command, so that what is seen was not made out of what was visible (Hebrews 11:3).

FAITH is the currency with which you are able to transact business in the unseen realm of God. Remember, the things which are seen were made from things not yet visible! Remember, *"For since the creation of the world God's invisible qualities—his eternal power and divine nature—have been clearly seen, being understood from what has been made, so that people are without excuse"* (Rom. 1:20).

Take Away for Today

1. Do you regularly conduct business in the unseen realm of God?

2. Do you believe that the universe was formed at God's command? What do you say to those who don't?

THE WORD BRINGS INCREASE

So the word of God spread. The number of disciples in Jerusalem increased rapidly, and a large number of priests became obedient to the faith (Acts 6:7).

A S the word spread, the number of disciples increased. Anything you speak the Word to will increase. Anything you speak the Word to will align with destiny and the purpose of God! After all, Jesus is the Word, *"In the beginning was the Word, and the Word was with God, and the Word was God. He was with God in the beginning. Through him all things were made; without him nothing was made that has been made"* (John 1:1-3). Spread the Word!

Take Away for Today

1. Are you spreading the Word of God?
2. Are the number of disciples in your neighborhood increasing?
3. Are you aligning with your destiny and purpose?

HE IS RISEN!

*From that time on Jesus began to explain to his disciples that he must go to Jerusalem and suffer many things at the hands of the elders, the chief priests and the teachers of the law, and that he must be killed and **on the third day be raised to life*** (Matthew 16:21).

THE grave could not hold Him. He conquered death! The power of His resurrection lies within you. The resurrection power is at work within you! If the same Spirit and power that raised the dead body of Jesus Christ to life lives in you, then you are an overcomer! From now on you will live in victory and the blessedness of our Christ!

Take Away for Today

1. How do you celebrate Easter?
2. Why is it important celebrate the reality of the risen Lord and Savior?

DON'T LOOK BACK

*If they had been thinking of the country they had left, they
would have had opportunity to return* (Hebrews 11:15).

D ON'T look back at the things you have left behind in the world
or you will be tempted. The danger of looking back or focusing on the past is the temptation to go backward! The Bible says had
they looked back they would have gone backward. On the way to the
Promised Land—a land flowing up with milk and honey—the Israelites remembered the garlic and the onions they had in Egypt, a land
of slavery. May you overcome the attraction of the past.

Take Away for Today

1. Is there something or someone in your past that you
   should let go but have not?

2. Do you frequently look to your past as being better than
   your future?

GOD BRINGS LIFE AND INCREASE

*And so from this one man, and he **as good as dead**, came descendants as numerous as the stars in the sky and as countless as the sand on the seashore* (Hebrews 11:12).

THE Bible describes Abraham at a time in his old age "as good as dead." Yet out of the loins of this man came descendants as numerous as the stars of the sky. God brings life and increase, *"Then Jesus looked up and said, 'Father, I thank you that you have heard me. I knew that you always hear me, but I said this for the benefit of the people standing here, that they may believe that you sent me.' When he had said this, Jesus called in a loud voice, 'Lazarus, come out!' The dead man came out..."* (John 11:41-44). May God bring fruitfulness out of every dead situation around you!

Take Away for Today

1. Do you sometimes feel dead inside?
2. Do you then eat of God's fruit and become alive in body, mind, and spirit?
3. Do you then listen for the voice of Jesus telling you to "Come out!"?

LIFE IS DECISION-DRIVEN

By faith Moses' parents hid him for three months after he was born, because they saw he was no ordinary child, and they were not afraid of the king's edict. By faith Moses, when he had grown up, refused to be known as the son of Pharaoh's daughter (Hebrews 11:23-24).

BECAUSE Moses was not an ordinary child, his parents decided to hide him. When Moses had grown, he chose not to be known as the son of Pharaoh's daughter. Life is the consequence of our decisions! Righteous decisions will move you toward your destiny, advancing you as you make progress in achieving your goals. Ungodly and selfish decisions will cause you to stumble backward. Choose wisely. Moses' parents made the decision that preserved his life. Moses, when he was grown up, made a decision to stick with God's people instead of the pleasure of Pharaoh's palace. Had he decided otherwise, he would not have entered his destiny in God. Indeed life is decision-driven!

Take Away for Today

1. Do you usually make the right decisions?
2. Do you remember a time(s) when you made a wrong decision and the consequences were unpleasant?

CONSIDER HIM

*Looking unto Jesus, the author and finisher of our faith, who for the joy that was set before Him endured the cross, despising the shame, and has sat down at the right hand of the throne of God. For **consider Him** who endured such hostility from sinners against Himself, lest you become weary and discouraged in your souls* (Hebrews 12:2-3).

JESUS came to this world that we may have life abundantly. One of the ways we can believe this is to fix our focus on Him and live above the circumstances that may surround us. Consider all He endured and don't grow weary. Consider all He suffered and don't grow apathetic. Consider all He taught and don't give up. Consider all He enjoyed and don't become disparaging. Consider Jesus.

Take Away for Today

1. Jesus looked beyond the cross to the joy set before Him. Can you do the same?

2. Do you easily become weary and discouraged?

NO EXCUSES!

And what more shall I say? I do not have time to tell about Gideon, Barak, Samson, Jephthah, David, Samuel and the prophets, who through faith conquered kingdoms, administered justice, and gained what was promised; who shut the mouths of lions, quenched the fury of the flames, and escaped the edge of the sword; whose weakness was turned to strength; and who became powerful in battle and routed foreign armies. Women received back their dead, raised to life again. Others were tortured and refused to be released, so that they might gain a better resurrection (Hebrews 11:32-35).

READ the Bible, think of the people of old and all they accomplished. Armed with faith in God, you can fight the fight of life! Let the success of others spur you to achieve greater heights in life. Today people are too ready to give excuses, complain, or blame others for their current situation rather than shutting the mouths of lions (taking charge of their lives) and quenching the fury of the flames (taking steps to improve their lot in life).

Take Away for Today

1. People who lived in Bible times were no different from modern-day believers. Do you have faith enough to conquer kingdoms, administer justice and gain what was promised?

2. Are you ready to shut the mouths of lions, quench the flames, and receive back the dead?

THOSE WHO BELONG TO GOD HEAR HIM

Whoever belongs to God hears what God says. The reason you do not hear is that you do not belong to God (John 8:47).

COULD it be so simple that we all miss the basic truth in this Scripture verse? If people do not belong to God, they are not entitled to hear Him. Any circumstance or sin that takes you away from God hinders your ability to hear from Him. Move close to God, and His voice will be clear to you.

Take Away for Today

1. Do you belong to God?
2. Do you hear His voice?

SET FREE BY THE TRUTH

Then you will know the truth, and the truth will set you free
(John 8:32).

THE truth has power! No limitation can hold back the power of the truth. Today if you are at a loss about which way to go, always choose the path of truth no matter how it seems; it is guaranteed to see you through.

Take Away for Today

1. How do you know what the truth is? What is your measuring device?

2. How does truth have power? What does that phrase mean to you?

_____

_____

_____

OVERWHELMED—YET HIS WILL PREVAILS

Then he said to them, "My soul is overwhelmed with sorrow to the point of death. Stay here and keep watch with me." Going a little farther, he fell with his face to the ground and prayed, "My Father, if it is possible, may this cup be taken from me. Yet not as I will, but as you will" (Matthew 26:38-39).

JESUS said though He was overwhelmed with sorrow even to the point of death—yet He still preferred that the will of God be done. This should be our prayer at all times that God's will be done. No matter the situation we are going through.

Take Away for Today

1. Does your will and God's will struggle at times? Which usually wins?

2. Does Jesus' prayer in Matthew 26 make it easier to relate to Him? Does it make you realize that even facing a death sentence, God's will is better than your own?

_____

_____

_____

FOR THIS REASON
I WAS BORN

*"You are a king, then!" said Pilate. Jesus answered, "You say that I am a king. In fact, **the reason I was born** and came into the world is to **testify to the truth.** Everyone on the side of truth listens to me" (John 18:37).*

THERE is always a reason behind a thing. Often this may clear in the heat of the happenings particularly if things seem to be complete contradictions to the perceived reason. Always seek the true reason behind what is happening in your life. Jesus said in the face of death, there is a reason, a divine plan behind the crucifixion! God will take the glory in your life.

Take Away for Today

1. Do you know the reason you were born?
2. Do you try and find the reason behind circumstances in your life?

_____

_____

_____

IT IS FINISHED—COMPLETELY PAID

*When he had received the drink, Jesus said, "It is finished." With
that, he bowed his head and gave up his spirit (John 19:30).*

IT is finished means paid in full! Your atonement, my atonement
was fully completed! If we accept Jesus Christ, it means all our
sins are washed—we are redeemed, purchased by His blood! All the
penalties that should have stood against us were nailed to the cross.
He paid for our sins in full; "it is finished."

Take Away for Today

1. What thoughts come to mind as you contemplate Jesus
   dying on the cross to save you?

2. How many sins did the blood of Jesus wash out of your
   life?

THE ARMOR OF LIGHT

The night is nearly over; the day is almost here. So let us put aside the deeds of darkness and put on the armor of light. Let us behave decently, as in the daytime, not in orgies and drunkenness, not in sexual immorality and debauchery, not in dissension and jealousy (Romans 13:12-13).

LIGHT has armor! Light has fruit! Whenever you choose light rather than darkness, you come into God's protection and fruitfulness. Whenever you put off the deeds of darkness—drunkenness, sexual immorality, jealousy and bitterness—you tap into the armor of life. Today choose the deeds of Light, not darkness!

Take Away for Today

1. Why do you think this verse associates night time with evilness?

2. Do you make it a practice to "behave decently"?

A Good Report – A Bright Hope For Tomorrow!

Then the two men started back. They went down out of the hills, forded the river and came to Joshua son of Nun and told him everything that had happened to them. They said to Joshua, "The Lord has surely given the whole land into our hands; all the people are melting in fear because of us" (Joshua 2:23-24).

T HESE spies brought good news to Joshua and the rest of Israel. Although their spy mission was riddled with life-threatening dangers, they chose instead to dwell on the positive—a bright hope for tomorrow! The joyful expectation of what tomorrow holds is the reason we are able to face each and every day.

Take Away for Today

1. When faced with challenges, even life-threatening dangers, do you choose to dwell on the positive?
2. Do you consistently hold in your heart and mind a bright hope for tomorrow?

OUR VICTORIES
SHOULD GLORIFY GOD

This is how you will know that the living God is among you and that he will certainly drive out before you the Canaanites, Hittites, Hivites, Perizzites, Girgashites, Amorites and Jebusites. See, the ark of the covenant of the Lord of all the earth will go into the Jordan ahead of you. Now then, choose twelve men from the tribes of Israel, one from each tribe. And as soon as the priests who carry the ark of the Lord—the Lord of all the earth—set foot in the Jordan, its waters flowing downstream will be cut off and stand up in a heap (Joshua 3:10-13).

O N this occasion they were instructed to let the Ark of the Lord go first. That means we should "Seek first the kingdom of God and all other things will be added to it"! Their victory—your victory—revealed that the living God was among them—within you.

Take Away for Today

1. Do you seek first the kingdom of God?
2. Are all other things added to you after you seek God first?

PROMOTION COMES FROM GOD

And the Lord said to Joshua, "Today I will begin to exalt you in the eyes of all Israel, so they may know that I am with you as I was with Moses" That day the Lord exalted Joshua in the sight of all Israel; and they revered him all the days of his life, just as they had revered Moses (Joshua 3:7; 4:14 NLT).

INDEED promotion and validation comes from God! Whatever you are going through, may the Lord validate and promote you to show His presence in your life. Some are afraid of promotion, thinking they can't assume the added responsibilities. Some are not confident enough to step out in faith. But the Lord says He will exalt you! Take that step of faith and you will be revered and admired.

Take Away for Today

1. Are you one to be revered, respected? What do you do to earn reverence and respect?

2. Has God stepped in to exalt you in the eyes of your family, your co-workers, your employer?

Have Faith, Please God

Now when Joshua was near Jericho, he looked up and saw a man standing in front of him with a drawn sword in his hand. Joshua went up to him and asked, "Are you for us or for our enemies?" "Neither," he replied, "but as commander of the army of the Lord I have now come." Then Joshua fell facedown to the ground in reverence, and asked him, "What message does my Lord have for his servant?" The commander of the Lord's army replied, "Take off your sandals, for the place where you are standing is holy." And Joshua did so (Joshua 5:13-15).

JOSHUA was doing most things right in the eyes of God, but when he drew near to Jericho and saw the wall, secretly his faith started to dwindle. The Living Bible translation says Joshua was sizing up the Jericho wall, which he was not meant to do. That allows doubts to come into the fickle human mind and even Joshua fell for this! Whatever wall is in front you today, know for sure the Lord who has brought you this far will see you through.

Take Away for Today

1. Do you allow your fickle human mind to entertain doubts and fears?

2. How can you keep your mind free from doubts and fears?

_____

_____

_____

Reading the Bible in a Year: 1 Kings 10-11 and Luke 24:1-35.

IF GOD BE FOR YOU

The Lord said to Joshua, "Stand up! What are you doing down on your face? Israel has sinned; they have violated my covenant, which I commanded them to keep. They have taken some of the devoted things; they have stolen, they have lied, they have put them with their own possessions. That is why the Israelites cannot stand against their enemies; they turn their backs and run because they have been made liable to destruction. I will not be with you anymore unless you destroy whatever among you is devoted to destruction" (Joshua 7:10-12).

THE Israelites had learned a great principle based on their incredible history mixed with outstanding testimonies. When they lost a battle, it was because God was angry with them—it was never about how strong the enemy was! If God be for you, who can be against you? When it comes down to the very bottom line, God is the only One who really matters. Focus on Him, not your possessions or even your friends and family—God will never turn His back on you.

Take Away for Today

1. Looking back over your life, have you learned this principle?

2. Have you learned that it matters not how strong your enemy is—God is stronger?

Reading the Bible in a Year: 1 Kings 12-13 and Luke 24:36-53.

THE VALLEY OF ACHOR

Then Joshua, together with all Israel, took Achan son of Zerah, the silver, the robe, the gold wedge, his sons and daughters, his cattle, donkeys and sheep, his tent and all that he had, to the Valley of Achor. Joshua said, "Why have you brought this trouble on us? The Lord will bring trouble on you today..."
(Joshua 24-25).

THE Valley of Achor is the place of judgment and punishment. This where the stern side of God was revealed for the Israelites to see. When people disobey God, there are consequences. Although we serve a merciful God who loves us dearly, He expects His children to obey Him—because His commands are always for our good, not for our detriment.

Take Away for Today

1.   Have you felt the consequences of disobeying God?
2.   Have you brought trouble upon yourself?

FROM THE VALLEY OF ACHOR TO A DOOR OF HOPE

Therefore I am now going to allure her; I will lead her into the desert and speak tenderly to her. There I will give her back her vineyards, and will make the Valley of Achor a door of hope. There she will sing as in the days of her youth, as in the day she came up out of Egypt (Hosea 2:14-15).

B Y the mercy of God and His infinite benevolence, every Valley of Achor can be turned into a door of hope. All we must do to enter the door of hope is confess our sins, repent, and ask the God of second chances to have mercy. He is ever faithful to hear us when we call on Him for forgiveness.

Take Away for Today

1. Are you knocking on the door of hope? Are you confident that He will open it for you?
2. Are you longing to hear God speak to you tenderly and receive from Him what you lost when you were in the valley?

_____

_____

_____

THEY DID NOT INQUIRE
OF THE LORD

The Israelites sampled their provisions but did not inquire of the Lord. Then Joshua made a treaty of peace with them to let them live, and the leaders of the assembly ratified it by oath. Three days after they made the treaty with the Gibeonites, the Israelites heard that they were neighbors, living near them. So the Israelites set out and on the third day came to their cities: Gibeon, Kephirah, Beeroth and Kiriath Jearim. But the Israelites did not attack them, because the leaders of the assembly had sworn an oath to them by the Lord, the God of Israel (Joshua 9:14-18).

P EOPLE look on the outside and judge others, but God sees what lies beneath the surface. That is why we must rely on the guidance of Him who does not fail. Make sure whatever is good is also of God! There are false prophets and evil doers of every kind in the world today. Always inquire of the Lord before making important decisions.

Take Away for Today

1. Are you apt to make quick judgments about people based on their clothing or speech?

2. Something may seem good, but it is always best to inquire of the Lord before making a decision or oath. Do you follow this advice?

Reading the Bible in a Year: 1 Kings 19-20 and John 2.

THE SUN AND THE MOON STOOD STILL

On the day the Lord gave the Amorites over to Israel, Joshua said to the Lord in the presence of Israel: "Sun, stand still over Gibeon, and you, moon, over the Valley of Aijalon." So the sun stood still, and the moon stopped, till the nation avenged itself on its enemies, as it is written in the Book of Jashar. The sun stopped in the middle of the sky and delayed going down about a full day. There has never been a day like it before or since, a day when the Lord listened to a human being. Surely the Lord was fighting for Israel! (Joshua 10:12-14)

O N the day of your power, maximize your efforts and do not let the momentum slip away without total victory. Joshua made an incredible command of the sun and moon to extend daylight until he declared victory over his enemies. You too can extend light and life over your battle grounds—at home, at work, at school, even at church—until you emerge victorious!

Take Away for Today

1. Why do you think the Lord listened to Joshua and granted his demand?
2. Do you have any doubt that this phenomenon happened just as the Bible states?

Reading the Bible in a Year: 1 Kings 21-22 and John 3:1-21.

TODAY IS MOTHER'S DAY!

Jesus replied, "'You shall not murder, you shall not commit adultery, you shall not steal, you shall not give false testimony, honor your father and mother,' and 'love your neighbor as yourself'" (Matthew 19:18-19).

A day set aside to honor our mothers—the woman who welcomed us into the world. We honor all mothers today and always. Truly the hand that rocks the cradle rules the world. Mothers rule the world! Mothers, I salute you. You deserve the best!

Take Away for Today

1. Do you have a good relationship with your mother? Why or why not?

2. Is there anything you can to today to brighten your mother's day—or someone who is close to you as a mother?

3. Is there something you need to forgive your mother for? Or something you need to ask her forgiveness for?

_____

_____

_____

FINISH YOUR DIVINE ASSIGNMENT

But the Israelites did not drive out the people of Geshur and Maacah, so they continue to live among the Israelites to this day (Joshua 13:13).

Judah could not dislodge the Jebusites, who were living in Jerusalem; to this day the Jebusites live there with the people of Judah (Joshua 15:63).

They did not dislodge the Canaanites living in Gezer; to this day the Canaanites live among the people of Ephraim but are required to do forced labor (Joshua 16:10).

Yet the Manassites were not able to occupy these towns, for the Canaanites were determined to live in that region. However, when the Israelites grew stronger, they subjected the Canaanites to forced labor but did not drive them out completely (Joshua 17:12-13).

I N all the above passages or stories, the Israelites failed to complete their divine assignments; and in the end, these unfinished assignments became a reproach to the future generation. Don't let the sun go down too many more times without considering your divine assignment and how you are progressing toward fulfilling it.

Take Away for Today

1. Have you asked the Lord what your divine assignment is?
2. Have you been journeying throughout life progressing toward fulfilling your divine assignment?

GOLIATH VERSUS
THE GOD OF ISRAEL

He said to David, "Am I a dog, that you come at me with sticks?" And the Philistine cursed David by his gods. "Come here," he said, "and I'll give your flesh to the birds of the air and the beasts of the field!" David said to the Philistine, "You come against me with sword and spear and javelin, but I come against you in the name of the Lord Almighty, the God of the armies of Israel, whom you have defied. This day the Lord will hand you over to me, and I'll strike you down and cut off your head. Today I will give the carcasses of the Philistine army to the birds of the air and the beasts of the earth, and the whole world will know that there is a God in Israel. All those gathered here will know that it is not by sword or spear that the Lord saves; for the battle is the Lord's, and he will give all of you into our hands" (1 Samuel 17:43-47).

GOLIATH was a giant, he was very powerful, and he had track records of successes—but no matter the strength, whoever comes against the God of Israel will fail! Like David, you too can face your foes with confidence knowing that the battle is the Lord's and He will save you.

Take Away for Today

1. Do you know arrogant people who think they can overpower your God?

2. How do you react to such people?

ASK AND YOU WILL RECEIVE

Now Zelophehad son of Hepher, the son of Gilead, the son of Makir, the son of Manasseh, had no sons but only daughters, whose names were Mahlah, Noah, Hoglah, Milcah and Tirzah. They went to Eleazar the priest, Joshua son of Nun, and the leaders and said, "The Lord commanded Moses to give us an inheritance among our relatives." So Joshua gave them an inheritance along with the brothers of their father, according to the Lord's command (Joshua 17:3-4).

AS mentioned on a previous day, receiving rests on a tripod of dimensions: 1) desire to have it; 2) the request to have it; and, 3) the preparedness to accommodate what is expected! When asking God for something, do you consider all the aspects of actually receiving what you expect?

Take Away for Today

1. Do you have a desire for it?
2. Did you make the request?
3. Are you prepared to receive?

THE LORD—OUR EXCEEDINGLY GREAT REWARD

The Lord gave them rest on every side, just as he had sworn to their ancestors. Not one of their enemies withstood them; the Lord handed all their enemies into their hands. Not one of all the Lord's good promises to the house of Israel failed; every one was fulfilled (Joshua 21:44-45).

THE greatest blessing on earth is the atoning blood of Jesus Christ. Whoever receives the Son receives the Kingdom of God and its infinite power and benevolence. Receiving the gift of redemption through Christ's sacrifice is the most important gift a person can experience. All of the Lord's good promises have been fulfilled. Hallelujah!

Take Away for Today

1. Have you accepted the Lord's good rest?
2. Have you acknowledged the fact that the Lord's good promises are also for you?

THIS IS WHAT
IS REQUIRED OF YOU

*But be very careful to keep the commandment and the law
that Moses the servant of the Lord gave you: to love the Lord
your God, to walk in all his ways, to obey his commands, to
hold fast to him and to serve him with all your heart and all
your soul* (Joshua 22:5).

NOTHING is too hard for God but there conditions required of
us to bring the power of God into our situation, that is obedience to His commandment. Joshua makes it clear that we need to
obey the Lord's commandments, love the Lord, walk in the path He
directs, and serve Him with our total being. After He sacrificed His
only Son for us, these requirements are not unreasonable.

Take Away for Today

1. Are you fully committed to loving God, walking in all
   of His ways?

2. Are you willing to obey His commands?

3. Will you serve Him with all of your heart and soul?

WHAT IF THIS IS TO TEST YOU

"I will no longer drive out before them any of the nations Joshua left when he died. I will use them to test Israel and see whether they will keep the way of the Lord and walk in it as their forefathers did." The Lord had allowed those nations to remain; he did not drive them out at once by giving them into the hands of Joshua (Judges 2:21-23).

W E can pass through situations that test our faithfulness and commitment to the things of God. But all the time the God we serve knows the end from the beginning. He knows the end of the journey before we even start. Be assured He has all things in His capable and loving hands!

Take Away for Today

1. Do you like taking tests?
2. Do you think it is fair that God tests His children? Why or why not?

_____

_____

_____

THE GENERATION THAT DID NOT KNOW GOD

After that whole generation had been gathered to their fathers, another generation grew up, who knew neither the Lord nor what he had done for Israel (Judges 2:10).

ONE of the most important legacies we can leave behind for future generations is the testimony of how we overcame by the grace that Almighty God made available to us. It is critical that the next generation be aware of God and what He did for millions of people throughout the ages who found hope and love and mercy when they turned from evil and toward Jesus, the Son of God.

Take Away for Today

1. Are you sharing your testimony with your children, grandchildren, relatives near and far?

2. Have you shared your testimony about God's only begotten Son with everyone willing to listen?

CURSED!

"Curse Meroz," said the angel of the Lord. "Curse its people bitterly, because they did not come to help the Lord, to help the Lord against the mighty" (Judges 5:23).

NOT that God needs the help of mere humans, but they were cursed because they failed to do what the Lord God required of them! We live in New Testament times when we know that Jesus took all of our sins upon Him and we are now covered by His blood of redemption. But...that gives us no valid excuse to disobey or ignore the Lord when He makes a request of us.

Take Away for Today

1. Were you shocked when you read the passage in Judges 5:23? That God would curse the people?

2. Do you think God would curse people today? Why or why not?

WHERE ARE THE WONDERS?

Gideon replied, "but if the Lord is with us, why has all this happened to us? Where are all his wonders that our ancestors told us about when they said, 'Did not the Lord bring us up out of Egypt?'..." (Judges 6:13).

GOD has not become weak; neither have His hands become feeble! We need to position ourselves to see the wonders that He can do for those who trust Him and put their hope in Him. God is capable of performing miracles and wonders beyond our imaginations and dreams. His timing is always perfect—and we need to be alert to witness what He has to reveal to us.

Take Away for Today

1. Are you wondering where the wonders are that are promised in the Bible?

2. Have you positioned yourself to see the wonders?

NEMESIS

After Abimelech had governed Israel three years, God sent an evil spirit between Abimelech and the citizens of Shechem, who acted treacherously against Abimelech. God did this in order that the crime against Jerub-Baal's seventy sons, the shedding of their blood, might be avenged on their brother Abimelech and on the citizens of Shechem, who had helped him murder his brothers (Judges 9:22-24).

ABIMELECH thought he got away from his heinous crimes of killing his brothers, but the table turned against him. The very people who helped in his crimes now turned on him. His nemesis! Don't do evil because it is in your power to do so; because whatever people sow, that is what they will reap.

Take Away for Today

1.   Do you have friends who would turn on you under the right circumstances?
2.   Do you put righteous acts before acts of revenge?

GOD KNOWS YOU

A certain man of Zorah, named Manoah, from the clan of the Danites, had a wife who was childless, unable to give birth (Judges 13:2).

GREATER than Google map is the radar of God; no one can escape divine detection. God knows everything about you—even the minute details. Manoah had a problem but what he probably didn't know was that the things he was going through were known to God—from whom nothing is hidden.

Take Away for Today

1. Is it reassuring that God knows everything about you? Or intimidating?
2. If God knows you so well…how well do you know Him?

_____

_____

_____

EVERY PROMISE FROM GOD HAS A RULE OF LIFE

The angel of the Lord appeared to her and said, "You are barren and childless, but you are going to become pregnant and give birth to a son. Now see to it that you drink no wine or other fermented drink and that you do not eat anything unclean. You will become pregnant and have a son whose head is never to be touched by a razor because the boy is to be a Nazirite, dedicated to God from the womb. He will take the lead in delivering Israel from the hands of the Philistines." So Manoah asked him, "When your words are fulfilled, what is to be the rule that governs the boy's life and work?" (Judges 13:3-5,12).

THIS great promise was the signal that the bareness of Manoah's marriage would end and that the end of the collective captivity of Israel would begin. With this great expectation, they rightly asked for the rule of operation of the promise when it is fulfilled.

Take Away for Today

1. Are you following the rule of life that God set before you?

2. Where is the rule of life to be found?

_____

_____

_____

ANGELS WORK
IN THE NAME OF GOD

Manoah said to the angel of the Lord, "We would like you to stay until we prepare a young goat for you." The angel of the Lord replied, "Even though you detain me, I will not eat any of your food. But if you prepare a burnt offering, offer it to the Lord." (Manoah did not realize that it was the angel of the Lord.) Then Manoah inquired of the angel of the Lord, "What is your name, so that we may honor you when your word comes true?" He replied, "Why do you ask my name? It is beyond understanding" (Judges 13:15-18).

ANGELS work in the name of the Lord and they do this so the glory will go to God and only God. Angels are not to be honored as God—they are God's messengers and deserve respect as such, nothing more. It is wrong to put angels on the same level as the Godhead, as they are creations of God, not equal to Him. It is right to appreciate angels and the relationship they have with God and humanity.

Take Away for Today

1. There has been a cultural fad about angels—do you believe that people were, or are, giving more attention to angels than the Creator of the angels?

2. Have you ever been helped or instructed by an angel?

3. Have you experienced the presence of an angel? What was your response?

GOD WILL NOT FORSAKE YOU

When the angel of the Lord did not show himself again to Manoah and his wife, Manoah realized that it was the angel of the Lord. "We are doomed to die!" he said to his wife. "We have seen God!" But his wife answered, "If the Lord had meant to kill us, he would not have accepted a burnt offering and grain offering from our hands, nor shown us all these things or now told us this" (Judges 13:21-23).

THE promise has enough divine and prophetic substance on which to anchor your life. When God promises you something in the future, it means God will protect you to fulfill His promise.

Take Away for Today

1. Has God promised you something in the future? Has He provided protection until that promise was fulfilled?
2. What is the difference between the Lord and the angel of the Lord?

THE WICKED GIVE BIRTH TO LIES

The wicked conceive evil; they are pregnant with trouble and give birth to lies. They dig a deep pit to trap others, then fall into it themselves. The trouble they make for others backfires on them. The violence they plan falls on their own heads (Psalm 7:14-16 NLT).

SOMETIMES it seems as if the wicked and evil people of the world come out ahead of those who are good and righteous. But that is not so. God has the last word about who comes out on top. Never forget that truth.

Take Away for Today

1. Have you witnessed times when it seems that people with no scruples or morals are more successful than good people who try to follow God's commandments?

2. Can you put trust in this Scripture passage that He is a just and fair Judge when the time comes?

THE LORD LEFT HIM

Then she called, "Samson, the Philistines are upon you!" He awoke from his sleep and thought, "I'll go out as before and shake myself free." But he did not know that the Lord had left him (Judges 16:20).

S AMSON put himself into a seriously dangerous predicament— one that God did not approve of or condone. Do not take the presence of God for granted! It is my sincere prayer that you will be sensitive to the Holy Spirit so that the Lord will never leave you.

Take Away for Today

1. What did Samson do to cause the Lord to leave him?
2. Because the Holy Spirit lives within you, be aware of His presence and do nothing to cause Him to grieve.

_____

_____

_____

Do Not Sin Against the Lord

So he said to them, "Why do you do such things? I hear from all the people about these wicked deeds of yours. No, my sons; the report I hear spreading among the Lord's people is not good. If one person sins against another, God may mediate for the offender; but if anyone sins against the Lord, who will intercede for them?" His sons, however, did not listen to their father's rebuke, for it was the Lord's will to put them to death
(1 Samuel 2:23-25).

E LI did not control his sons firmly and allowed them in position of authority, which led to their deaths. Eli may have found himself in a situation that many parents know all too well today—trying to control wayward children. Parents must intercede for their children, but when they are rebuked, the children will suffer the consequences. When anyone sins against the Lord, Jesus will intercede for them—if asked.

Take Away for Today

1. Have unruly children caused pain and suffering in your family or the family of someone you know?
2. What is the best way to handle such situations?

THE WORST OF ALL FAMINES

The boy Samuel ministered before the Lord under Eli. In those days the word of the Lord was rare; there were not many visions (1 Samuel 3:1).

THIS is the worst of all famines! A famine usually refers to food, but this famine was starving the people of visions from the Lord. His word to the people "was rare," so they didn't know what was on His mind. They were spiritually blind. Spiritual blindness is groping in the darkness of life without God. That is why the Bible says the people perish for lack of vision.

Take Away for Today

1. Is your church or ministry suffering from spiritual blindness?
2. Are you?

_____

_____

_____

You Can Grow in Favor with God

The Lord was with Samuel as he grew up, and he let none of his words fall to the ground. And all Israel from Dan to Beersheba recognized that Samuel was attested as a prophet of the Lord. The Lord continued to appear at Shiloh, and there he revealed himself to Samuel through his word (1 Samuel 3:19-21).

THE more you move close to God, the more the favor of God in your life. Favor is the divine advantage in the situation. Moving closer to God means reading and absorbing His Word, praising and worshiping Him, and loving one another. May you grow in favor with God.

Take Away for Today

1. What does the Scripture mean that God let none of Samuel's words fall to the ground?

2. What can you do to gain or earn God's favor?

THE DANGER OF PRESUMPTION

When the soldiers returned to camp, the elders of Israel asked, "Why did the Lord bring defeat upon us today before the Philistines? Let us bring the ark of the Lord's covenant from Shiloh, so that it may go with us and save us from the hand of our enemies" (1 Samuel 4:3).

I T was presumptuous to think the physical presence of the Ark of Covenant was more important than getting right with God. God can fight from afar as well as from near. We don't always know what the Lord wants us to do in a particular situation. It is always best to pray to Him for direction.

Take Away for Today

1. Do you have a presumptuous nature? Has this caused problems for you?
2. Do you presume the worst? The best?

A SENSE OF PURPOSE

He has made everything beautiful in its time. He also has planted eternity in men's hearts and minds [a divinely implanted sense of a purpose working through the ages which nothing under the sun but God alone can satisfy], yet so that men cannot find out what God has done from the beginning to the end (Ecclesiastes 3:11 AMP).

GOD'S purpose is within your heart and secured from the enemy of your soul. Only you and God can reach it. Knowing that God made everything beautiful according to His perfect timing should be very comforting. Knowing that He planted His divine purpose in our hearts and minds should be even more comforting and should motivate us to search our hearts and minds to discover our destiny.

Take Away for Today

1. Do you believe that God has divinely implanted a specific purpose within you?

2. Have you sought and found your purpose and are you walking forward in it daily?

_____

_____

_____

GOD'S UNTOUCHABLES

*You'll be built solid, grounded in righteousness, far from any trouble—nothing to fear! Far from terror—it won't even come close! If anyone attacks you, don't for a moment suppose that I sent them, and if any should attack nothing will come of it. I create the blacksmith who fires up his forge and makes a weapon designed to kill. I also create the destroyer—but **no weapon that can hurt you has ever been forged.** Any accuser who takes you to court will be dismissed as a liar. This is what God's servants can expect. **I'll see to it that everything works out for the best** (Isaiah 54:11-17 The Message).*

THIS is a great promise; in other words, we are God's untouchables—solid in righteousness and far from troubles! God will work out everything for the best, and we need to stand firmly on this promise of His. Only He knows what is "best" for us—not our spouse, or our parents, or our pastor, although we need to heed their good advice discerningly.

Take Away for Today

1. Would you like to be "far from any trouble" and "far from terror"?

2. How can you make that happen? On your own? Or with God's help?

3. Can you accept in your heart and mind that God will work everything out for the best?

Reading the Bible in a Year: 2 Chronicles 7-9 and John 13:1-17.

DON'T DESPISE SMALL ASSIGNMENTS

Kish had a son named Saul, as handsome a young man as could be found anywhere in Israel, and he was a head taller than anyone else. Now the donkeys belonging to Saul's father Kish were lost, and Kish said to his son Saul, "Take one of the servants with you and go and look for the donkeys" (1 Samuel 9:2-3).

ALTHOUGH this might not have been a very honorable assignment, Saul obeyed his father and in the process found his destiny. This is a demonstration of the virtues of obedience. When you obey God, He blesses you and you move closer to your destiny. Sometimes you may not be aware of this progress toward your life's purpose, so don't dismiss any step forward that takes you in the right direction. Do not despise the days of small beginnings.

Take Away for Today

1. Do (or did) you obey your parents, even though you may have other ideas?
2. Did you find your destiny while in the process of obeying a parent or the Lord?

TOUGH MISSION DOESN'T MEAN WRONG MISSION

So he passed through the hill country of Ephraim and through the area around Shalisha, but they did not find them. They went on into the district of Shaalim, but the donkeys were not there. Then he passed through the territory of Benjamin, but they did not find them. When they reached the district of Zuph, Saul said to the servant who was with him, "Come, let's go back, or my father will stop thinking about the donkeys and start worrying about us." But the servant replied, "Look, in this town there is a man of God; he is highly respected, and everything he says comes true. Let's go there now. Perhaps he will tell us what way to take" (1 Samuel 9:4-6).

FOR Saul, the truth of God played out in front of him. Whatever your hands find to do, do it with all your strength. He thought he was obeying his father and just looking for the lost donkeys. This mission was not about donkeys at all, it was just the process of bringing Saul to his destiny.

Take Away for Today

1. When a project is hard, do you sometimes want to give up too soon?

2. Do you seek godly people for godly advice?

I AM THE SEER

"I am the seer," Samuel replied. "Go up ahead of me to the high place, for today you are to eat with me, and in the morning I will let you go and will tell you all that is in your heart. As for the donkeys you lost three days ago, do not worry about them; they have been found. And to whom is all the desire of Israel turned, if not to you and your whole family line?" (1 Samuel 9:19-20)

SAMUEL was Saul's destiny helper! Saul was looking for missing donkeys but he found the kingship and rulership over Israel. Samuel showed Saul the way and Saul accepted his assistance. Many times God places people in our lives to help us see Him more clearly. Be aware of who comes in and out of your circle of friends, family, co-workers, ministry helpers, etc. Be careful how you treat people that come across your path in life, you never know when a destiny helper comes along! A destiny helper for both Saul and Naaman came in form of a servant!

Take Away for Today

1. Do you have a destiny helper—someone who reveals God's will for your life?

2. When you position yourself in righteousness and have a willing spirit, will good things come to you and your family?

_____

_____

_____

UNCOMMON FAVOR

Samuel said to the cook, "Bring the piece of meat I gave you, the one I told you to lay aside." So the cook took up the thigh with what was on it and set it in front of Saul. Samuel said, "Here is what has been kept for you. Eat, because it was set aside for you for this occasion, from the time I said, 'I have invited guests.'" And Saul dined with Samuel that day (1 Samuel 9:23-24).

FAVOR is divine goodwill; and in this instance, Saul was favored by God to be the highest authority in Israel despite his humble origin. This kind of favor is uncommon because it turned a commoner into royalty. On this occasion Saul received the reserved and the choicest portion. Whatever the Lord has reserved for you, you will receive it and prosper in it!

Take Away for Today

1.   God can turn anyone of any status into royalty. Are you ready to wear your crown?

2.   Do you readily accept goodwill from others? To extend goodwill to others?

HEARTS THE LORD
HAS TOUCHED

Saul also went to his home in Gibeah, accompanied by valiant men whose hearts God had touched (1 Samuel 10:26).

ONLY the Holy Spirit can change a person! When Gods says, "men whose hearts" the Lord has touched, means those who have been prepared and delivered for a purpose. The heart of humanity is desperately wicked, who can understand it! So in ministries, one should ask God to send only those whom He has touched.

Take Away for Today

1. Can you discern between people the Lord as touched and those who haven't received a touch from Him?
2. Has your heart been touched by God?

_____

_____

_____

"AM I IN THE PLACE OF GOD?"

But Joseph said to them, "Don't be afraid. Am I in the place of God? You intended to harm me, but God intended it for good to accomplish what is now being done, the saving of many lives. So then, don't be afraid. I will provide for you and your children." And he reassured them and spoke kindly to them (Genesis 50:19-21).

"AM I in the place of God?" This is another profound statement from Joseph. Another is "Does not interpretation belong to God?" No one should take the place of God in any of our utterances. The fact that you have power does not mean reckless use, because "all power belongs to God." Some people unconsciously assume the place of God without knowing because of the power bestowed on them by God. Like Joseph we should all consciously enthrone God in every area of our lives. Sometimes, events and people may tend to push us in to such position as though we have absolute power. But all power belongs to God from whom all blessings flow.

Take Away for Today

1. Do you know people who seem to think they are equal to or at least closer to God than you are?

2. When you speak, is it with kindness and with a humble spirit?

NEVER GIVE UP ON GOD

"What was it he said to you?" Eli asked. "Do not hide it from me. May God deal with you, be it ever so severely, if you hide from me anything he told you." So Samuel told him everything, hiding nothing from him. Then Eli said, "He is the Lord; let him do what is good in his eyes" (1 Samuel 3:17-18).

I T is true that Eli's children had given him hard times and they were out of his control, but in God we must always have hope! Eli was told that grave punishment would befall his family and his wayward children, and he chose not to intercede! Perhaps he might have done so in the past on countless occasions. Nevertheless, Eli gave up on redeeming his family. We should never give up on God. No matter what, God is a compassionate God. Don't write off God's grace of a second chance. Don't give up on your children!

Take Away for Today

1. Have you had trying times while raising your children?
2. Have you given up on your children, your marriage, your job?
3. Do you think God would ever give up on you? Are you grateful that He has given you a second, third... chance?

THE LORD CAN FIGHT
FOR HIMSELF

After the Philistines had captured the ark of God, they took it from Ebenezer to Ashdod. Then they carried the ark into Dagon's temple and set it beside Dagon. When the people of Ashdod rose early the next day, there was Dagon, fallen on his face on the ground before the ark of the Lord! They took Dagon and put him back in his place. But the following morning when they rose, there was Dagon, fallen on his face on the ground before the ark of the Lord! His head and hands had been broken off and were lying on the threshold; only his body remained (1 Samuel 5:1-4).

THE Philistines thought the battle was over but they soon learned it had only just begun! God can fight for Himself! Indeed, the battle is not over until it is over! For instance, the devil thought and rejoiced that Jesus was crucified on the cross, but in reality Jesus went to the grave for divine purpose—defeat the power of death. Don't give up the fight!

Take Away for Today

1. Has God brought you victory when you thought all was lost?

2. Do you give God the benefit of the doubt, knowing that He is the Victor in every situation?

_____

_____

GOD ALONE
CAN DELIVER THIS WAY!

Make models of the tumors and of the rats that are destroying the country, and give glory to Israel's god. Perhaps he will lift his hand from you and your gods and your land (1 Samuel 6:5).

HERE it is: God is supreme and sovereign in all the land. The hand of God was heavy on the Philistines, their god and their land and the whole people submitted to the God of Israel after an undisputed silent warfare; no arrow was shot, no gun was fired, and no chariot moved—yet the whole enemy nation submitted to the God of the Hebrews.

Take Away for Today

1. God sometimes uses nature and human nature to win the battle. Are you sensitive to His movements among your people and nation?

2. Have you ever felt the heavy hand of God upon your life and changed your ways?

_____

_____

_____

AVOID HUMILIATION

Don't work yourself into the spotlight; don't push your way into the place of prominence. It's better to be promoted to a place of honor than face humiliation by being demoted (Proverbs 25:6-7 The Message).

RATHER than seeking the spotlight, put yourself humbly where you can do the most good, and you will eventually be noticed and brought forward to where God thinks best. As Jesus said, "When someone invites you to a wedding feast, do not take the place of honor, for a person more distinguished than you may have been invited. If so, the host who invited both of you will come and say to you, 'Give this person your seat.' Then, humiliated, you will have to take the least important place." May we be wise enough to avoid humiliation.

Take Away for Today

1. Have you been humiliated in front of a crowd or someone you knew?

2. Could this humiliation have been avoided if you were more humble?

GOD HAS RESERVED THE CHOICEST FOR YOU

Samuel said to the cook, "Bring the piece of meat I gave you, the one I told you to lay aside." So the cook took up the leg with what was on it and set it in front of Saul. Samuel said, "Here is what has been kept for you. Eat, because it was set aside for you for this occasion, from the time I said, 'I have invited guests.'" And Saul dined with Samuel that day (1 Samuel 9:23-24).

WHAT God reserved for you will wait for you. This is how the Living Bible says it: *"Samuel then instructed the chef to bring Saul the choicest cut of meat, the piece that had been set aside for the guest of honor. So the chef brought it in and placed it before Saul. 'Go ahead and eat it,' Samuel said, 'for I was saving it for you, even before I invited these others!' So Saul ate with Samuel"* (1 Samuel 9:23-24). When God sets something aside for you, no enemy can take it; and at the appropriate time, your manifestation will come through.

Take Away for Today

1. What do you think the Lord has set aside for you?

2. In your spirit can you imagine what fantastic blessings He has been keeping for you—waiting for the perfect occasion to present them to you?

_____

_____

_____

Reading the Bible in a Year: Ezra 3-5 and John 20.

PRIDE, FEAR, AND PRESUMPTION

[Saul said] I thought, "Now the Philistines will come down against me at Gilgal, and I have not sought the Lord's favor." So I felt compelled to offer the burnt offering. "You acted foolishly," Samuel said. "You have not kept the command the Lord your God gave you; if you had, he would have established your kingdom over Israel for all time" (1 Samuel 13:12-13).

THIS was a great mistake on the part of Saul, we should learn from this. We should not allow people, circumstance, or pressure to compel us to disobey God. Saul was too quick to try and solve his problem and it cost him his kingdom and the Lord's favor. Under pressure, Saul assumed the role of the priest, tried to please God in an ungodly way, acted presumptuously and outside the remits of his kingship authority, and Samuel said he "acted foolishly." It is crucial that we seek the Lord and not act foolishly.

Take Away for Today

1. Has there been a time when you felt pressured into disobeying God? Did you give in to the pressure? How did it turn out?

2. Have you missed out on blessings from God because you disobeyed Him?

_____

_____

_____

THE LORD SAVES
BY MANY OR FEW

Jonathan said to his young armor-bearer, "Come, let's go over to the outpost of those uncircumcised men. Perhaps the Lord will act in our behalf. Nothing can hinder the Lord from saving, whether by many or by few" (1 Samuel 14:6).

THERE are two ways to see this situation revealed in the Scripture above. On one hand God can use many or few to do His purpose. On the other hand it does not matter how great the enemy's offensive is—God will not fail. God determines the outcome. Today, as for you, whether your strength is small or your challenge is enormous, it does not matter, it is God who counts!

Take Away for Today

1. In this modern age, God saves hundreds when they surrender to Him at revivals and mass outreaches—have you witnessed such?

2. Although God saves hundreds at a time, His reach is into every heart, personally connecting His with each new believer. Have you witnessed such?

DON'T LIVE IN THE PAST

The Lord said to Samuel, "How long will you mourn for Saul,
since I have rejected him as king over Israel? Fill your horn with
oil and be on your way; I am sending you to Jesse of Bethlehem.
I have chosen one of his sons to be king" (1 Samuel 16:1).

EVEN in the best hands, things or people may not turn out as expected; but life goes on and God is still in control! Samuel was disappointed in the way Saul turned out, but we serve a God of second chances. Samuel soon realized that even in this God had another plan to anoint David in place of Saul! God's plan cannot be thwarted! The Lord has a new, greater, and better assignment for you. Don't get caught up with what should have been. Fill your horn with oil, get up, your anointing still stands and there are lives to be saved. God has chosen you as one of His children. And His children are meant to do great things!

Take Away for Today

1. Are you still mourning the loss of a loved one? A divorce? A health problem?

2. Will you take the Lord's command to Samuel to heart and "be on your way" to forgetting the past and forging forward to a new plan for your life?

_____

_____

_____

DO YOU COME IN PEACE?

Samuel did what the Lord said. When he arrived at Bethlehem, the elders of the town trembled when they met him. They asked, "Do you come in peace?" (1 Samuel 16:4).

THE elders of the city met the prophet Samuel at the entrance and asked if he came in peace. If elders do not perform their role, they incur the wrath of God. Leaders in ministry need to be attuned to God in a very special way. They will be held accountable to the people and to God.

Take Away for Today

1. Do you have confidence in your spiritual leaders?
2. Do you pray for them regularly?
3. Do you believe they are ministering to the best of their ability and that the Lord's favor is upon them?

GOD LOOKS AT THE HEART

But the Lord said to Samuel, "Do not consider his appearance or his height, for I have rejected him. The Lord does not look at the things people look at. People look at the outward appearance, but the Lord looks at the heart" (1 Samuel 16:7).

LOOKS can be deceptive and things may not be what they seem to our natural eyes. It is wise to pray for discernment, especially in this age of mass communication and multimedia. Things and people can be deceiving yet seem right and true. Be very careful when looking at things and people from the outside only—search deeper and longer before believing. Trust God to show you the truth.

Take Away for Today

1. Do you take the time to look at people and circumstances with your spiritual eyes rather than your natural eyes?

2. Have you ever been "taken in" by an attractive and smooth-talking person?

3. Have you ever been "put off" by unattractive and shy people only to realize that they were absolutely wonderful people after getting to know them?

DOES AGE MATTER?

Jesse had seven of his sons pass before Samuel, but Samuel said to him, "The Lord has not chosen these." So he asked Jesse, "Are these all the sons you have?" "There is still the youngest," Jesse answered, "but he is tending the sheep." Samuel said, "Send for him; we will not sit down until he arrives." So he sent and had him brought in. He was ruddy, with a fine appearance and handsome features. Then the Lord said, "Rise and anoint him; he [David] is the one" (1 Samuel 16:10-12).

IN the natural, David could not possibly be the one! He was the youngest and the father did not think he would be the one. But the ceremony was suspended until he arrived and God anointed David the king! We may not think we are "the one" but in reality all of God's children are "the ones"! Let us act and think as winners—at every age.

Take Away for Today

1. When you were younger, did people take you as seriously as when you were more mature?
2. Do you tend to think older people are wiser?
3. Can you see the positive attributes in people of all ages?

THE HOLY SPIRIT
DRIVES OUT EVIL SPIRITS

Whenever the spirit from God came upon Saul, David would take his lyre and play. Then relief would come to Saul; he would feel better, and the evil spirit would leave him (1 Samuel 16:23).

WHEN the glory of God comes, evil spirits flee. Evil spirits exist today as well as back in biblical times. But we know that greater is the God in us than the evil that is in the world. Today make sure you allow the glory of God to permeate your atmosphere.

Take Away for Today

1. The Lord was with David and so could comfort King Saul. Do you have the gift to comfort others?

2. Do you know of those who can make evil spirits leave because they are filled with the Spirit of God?

3. Is this gift from God to comfort others one you have asked Him to give you?

_____

_____

_____

IT'S YOUR TIME

Jesus came back at them, "Don't crowd me. This isn't my time. It's your time—it's always your time; you have nothing to lose. The world has nothing against you, but it's up in arms against me. It's against me because I expose the evil behind its pretensions. You go ahead, go up to the Feast. Don't wait for me. I'm not ready. It's not the right time for me" (John 7:6-8 The Message).

AS mentioned previously, God's timing is perfect. Jesus knew this truth and it is what prompted His response to the disciples. He knew He wasn't ready; He told them to go ahead. Sometimes God leads us, as He did Moses in the wilderness, and sometimes He tells us to go ahead. No matter what is in front or behind us, He always has our best interests in hand and in heart.

Take Away for Today

1. Would you rather Jesus be ahead of you leading the way?
2. Or would you rather have Jesus behind you, protecting your back?

EACH WILL GIVE AN ACCOUNT

So then, each of us will give an account of ourselves to God
(Romans 14:12).

NOTHING is hidden from God, so be assured someday everyone will give account to God from whom nothing can be hidden—everything lays bare before Him. You may have thought of Ananias and Sapphira (see Acts 5:2-4) when you read the verse in Romans 14; it is good to remember that we will give an account of ourselves to God not only when we meet Him when we die, but He also keeps watch over us during our lifetimes.

Take Away for Today

1. Are you looking forward to the day when you stand before God and give your account to Him?

2. Are you dreading the day when you stand before God and give your account to Him?

GOD IS THE JUDGE

Who are you to judge someone else's servant? To their own master, servants stand or fall. And they will stand, for the Lord is able to make them stand (Romans 14:4).

DO not judge people, judgment belongs to God. If you judge, you too will be judged with the same standard. Too often people, including Christians, judge others without knowing the whole story or background of a situation. This is unfair to the person and puts you in a position that God never intended. Only He is the Judge—the only fair and just evaluator of a person's guilt or innocence.

Take Away for Today

1. Do you know people who make it their life mission to judge and convict others?

2. Do you tend to judge people according to your own set of rules and moral code?

3. Aren't you glad that God is merciful and judges fairly? Can you say the same for yourself?

PAY CAREFUL ATTENTION—DO NOT DRIFT AWAY

We must pay more careful attention, therefore, to what we have heard, so that we do not drift away (Hebrews 2:1).

DRIFTING from the values of Christianity is common; but what is important is that every time you drift from God, return to Him with a heart of repentance. The danger of drifting is that it can be subtle and may not be easily recognizable. That is why we must set values in our lives. Goals pull the vision to fulfillment and values help us keep the boundaries. Your values should alert you when you are drifting.

Take Away for Today

1. Have you set values for yourself that keep you safely under God's umbrella of safety and security?
2. Do you need to pay careful attention to what you have heard from God and have read in His Word so you don't drift away from His plan for your life?

JESUS IS THE SAME FOREVER

Jesus Christ is the same yesterday and today and forever
(Hebrews 13:8).

GOD is not a man we cannot depend on—God is God, and we can always depend on Him. He does not change; we can be confident of this, we can trust and rely on Him and His promises today and every day. When others let us down or disappoint us, we can rest assured that Jesus Christ loves and cares for us moment by moment.

Take Away for Today

1. Have others disappointed you because you depended on them and they didn't follow through?

2. Have others broken your trust or not kept their promises?

3. Have you realized the foolishness of depending on people rather than God—the God who is always faithful, trustworthy, and fulfills His promises?

A LOVE SO DEEP

See what great love the Father has lavished on us, that we should be called children of God! And that is what we are!...
(1 John 3:1)

G OD chose us and we are His people, the sheep of His pasture. When we were yet sinners, He sent His Son to die for us, which translated us into the light of His marvelous Kingdom. Jesus Christ took away our sins, our infirmities, and gave us peace within that passes all understanding! What a love so deep!

Take Away for Today

1. Have you accepted fully this deep and precious love from God?
2. How peaceful are you deep within yourself?
3. Can you fathom the depth of His love for you?

_____

_____

_____

HOPE DOES NOT DISAPPOINT

Now hope does not disappoint, because the love of God has been poured out in our hearts by the Holy Spirit who was given to us (Romans 5:5 NKJV).

KEEP your hope alive! In real terms it is the hope of a better tomorrow that gives us the zeal each and every new day. If you have the Holy Spirit then God has poured His love abroad in your heart. Although you may be in the middle of troubles and turmoil, you can always hope—hope is the flicker of light within dark circumstances. Hold on to hope, you won't be disappointed!

Take Away for Today

1.   Are you a hopeful person? Why or why not?
2.   Do you feel hope and peace and love in your heart—placed there by the Holy Spirit Himself?

REAL POWER IS FROM GOD

He was in the world, and though the world was made through him, the world did not recognize him. He came to that which was his own, but his own did not receive him. Yet to all who received him, to those who believed in his name, he gave the right to become children of God—children born not of natural descent, nor of human decision or a husband's will, but born of God (John 1:10-13).

BECOMING the children of God brings power. This is the real power because it emanates from the One who has all power. You have the power to overcome your debt, your bad temper, your marriage troubles, your unemployment status, your lack of confidence, and anything else keeping you from experiencing a super-abundant life in Christ.

Take Away for Today

1. Do you act and think as a powerful child of God?

2. Do you accept your role as a child of God with thankfulness or begrudgingly?

_____

_____

_____

CHOSEN PEOPLE

But you are a chosen people, a royal priesthood, a holy nation,
God's special possession, that you may declare the praises of
him who called you out of darkness into his wonderful light
(1 Peter 2:9).

W E are God's people because He chose us, we are His people,
the sheep of His pasture. It is good to praise Him because He
called us out of the darkness—He brought us into His glorious light
where we can see Him clearly and know that He is with us every
moment of every day.

Take Away for Today

1. Write First Peter 2:9 in your own words and expand the
    verse to include how you feel being chosen by God.

2. How do you declare the praises of God?

_____

_____

_____

THE SACRIFICE OF PRAISE—THE FRUIT OF THE LIPS

Through Jesus, therefore, let us continually offer to God a sacrifice of praise—the fruit of lips that openly profess his name (Hebrews 13:15).

Through Him, therefore, let us constantly and at all times offer up to God a sacrifice of praise, which is the fruit of lips that thankfully acknowledge and confess and glorify His name (Hebrews 13:15 AMP).

WHEN you think of the goodness of God and all that He has done for you, all you can say is, "Thank You, God!" This is what David said, *"God, make a fresh start in me, shape a Genesis week from the chaos of my life. Don't throw me out with the trash, or fail to breathe holiness in me. Bring me back from gray exile, put a fresh wind in my sails! Give me a job teaching rebels your ways so the lost can find their way home. Commute my death sentence, God, my salvation God, and I'll sing anthems to your life-giving ways. Unbutton my lips, dear God; I'll let loose with your praise"* (Psalm 51:10-15 The Message). May the Lord unbutton your lips to praise Him today!

Take Away for Today

1. What is your favorite way to thank and praise your heavenly Father?

2. Have your lips been unbuttoned and the fruit of your lips been used to nourish God's eyes and ears with worship of Him?

Reading the Bible in a Year: Job 19-20 and Acts 9:23-43.

Whatever is Good and Perfect Comes from God

Every good gift and every perfect gift is from above, and cometh down from the Father of lights, with whom is no variableness, neither shadow of turning (James 1:17 KJV).

THIS God is our God from now even to the end of time. He does not change nor has any shadow of doubt. His gifts make us rich and cause us no sorrow. Once He gives a gift He does not revoke it. He is not the author of confusion because He is the Father of Light.

Take Away for Today

1. When you receive a gift—of any kind—do you thank your heavenly Father who is ultimately the originator of your gift?
2. Do you see God as the Father of Light? If so you will never walk in darkness!

TEMPTATION IS THE PULL OF OUR EVIL THOUGHTS

And remember when someone wants to do wrong it is never God who is tempting him, for God never wants to do wrong and never tempts anyone else to do it. Temptation is the pull of man's own evil thoughts and wishes. These evil thoughts lead to evil action and afterward to the death penalty from God (James 1:13-15 TLB).

THOUGHTS are like seeds; if we sow a thought, we reap an idea that will crave for action. Evil thoughts can grip us intensely and they are often hard to break off. The power of evil thought can attract like a magnetic pull. Do not entertain evil thoughts so you will not be pulled away from God by them.

Take Away for Today

1. Do evil thoughts sometimes creep into your mind?
2. What do you do to combat the evil thoughts that invade your mind?
3. Have your evil thoughts ever led to evil action? What was the result?

_____

_____

_____

AN OPPORTUNITY TO GROW

Consider it pure joy, my brothers and sisters, whenever you face trials of many kinds, because you know that the testing of your faith produces perseverance. Let perseverance finish its work so that you may be mature and complete, not lacking anything (James 1:2-4).

I F you follow God faithfully, you will grow. Step by step God will take you to your destiny. God wants us to mature in Him so we can experience all that He has for us. This maturing may include testing our faith so we will learn how to persevere, which leads us to finishing, completing our calling and purpose on earth.

Take Away for Today

1. Has your faith been tested during trials and troubles?

2. Have you persevered through challenges that seemed to last for more than you thought you could endure?

3. Have you spiritually matured because of your perseverance?

_____

_____

_____

LISTEN THEN DO

Do not merely listen to the word, and so deceive yourselves.
Do what it says (James 1:22).

I F you hear His Word, then do what it says so that the truth of it can set you free. Doing the Word of God is like building a house with a solid foundation. On that solid foundation your house survives whatever comes against it. After you listen to God's Word and follow through, you will know the truth. There will be no deception when you obey God's Word.

Take Away for Today

1. How solid is the foundation of your spiritual home?

2. After reading His Word or hearing His word, do you follow through and *do* what it says?

BODY WITHOUT SPIRIT—FAITH WITHOUT DEEDS

As the body without the spirit is dead, so faith without deeds is dead (James 2:26).

THIS is incredible, the life of the body is its spirit. When the spirit leaves the body, the body becomes dead. The spirit gives the body its life from the very beginning. As the Bible says, *"Then the Lord God formed a man from the dust of the ground and breathed into his nostrils the breath of life, and the man became a living being"* (Gen. 2:7). This is the essence and the center of life on earth; that we should allow the rule of the Spirit to permeate the whole of our being. To be spiritually dead is to be distant from God and His Spirit.

Take Away for Today

1. If you are not filled with the Spirit, does that mean you are spiritually dead?
2. Have you asked God to breathe the breath of life into you?

JUSTIFIED BY GOOD DEEDS

You see that a man is justified (pronounced righteous before God) through what he does and not alone through faith [through works of obedience as well as by what he believes]. So also with Rahab the harlot—was she not shown to be justified (pronounced righteous before God) by [good] deeds when she took in the scouts (spies) and sent them away by a different route? (James 2:24-25 AMP)

FAITH is the assurance that what we hope for will come to pass, and for it to become complete by deeds. But we need to back up our faith with appropriate action. Rahab provided safe passage for God's spies. Rahab by her profession was condemned to death, but through faith backed up by good deeds she was redeemed. God will also provide opportunities for you to help His children in one way or another. Be ready to say yes! Put righteousness into action!

Take Away for Today

1. Do your faith and actions work together for the glory of God?
2. Is your faith made complete by what you do?
3. Are others convinced you are a child of God by watching your faith in action?

BREAD RETURNED TO THE HOUSE OF GOD

When Naomi heard in Moab that the LORD had come to the aid of his people by providing food for them, she and her daughters-in-law prepared to return home from there (Ruth 1:6).

B ETHLEHEM is the house of God. This passage confirms that no famine lasts forever, and sooner or later bread will return to the house of God. As indeed Naomi soon learned that God had provided for His people. Throughout the Bible, God provided for His people. In a variety of ways He revealed then and reveals now His compassion for those who love and obey Him. Provision will also return to your household as you show Him your devotion and obedience.

Take Away for Today

1. You can depend on God to provide for you and your family. Do you count on this promise of His?

2. The Lord comes to the aid of His people—has He come to your aid lately? In what way?

_____

_____

_____

STRANGE FIRE

*But Nadab and Abihu died when they made an offering
before the LORD with unauthorized fire)* (Numbers 26:61).

GOD will be put off by ungody fire. When the sons of Aaron
started a strange fire, God allowed it to consume them. *"For
the Lord your God is a consuming fire, a jealous God"* (Deut. 4:24).
Jesus said, *"Every plant that my heavenly father has not planted will
be pulled up by roots"* (Matt. 15:13). May the fire consume everything
not planted by God in your life.

Take Away for Today

1. Have you been placing strange offerings before God?
2. Will you allow God to burn all ungodliness in your life?
3. What is it about God being jealous that you may not
    understand?

BREAK DOWN THE EVIL ALTAR

This is what you are to do to them: Break down their altars, smash their sacred stones, cut down their Asherah poles and burn their idols in the fire. For you are a people holy to the Lord your God. The Lord your God has chosen you out of all the peoples on the face of the earth to be his people, his treasured possession (Deuteronomy 7:5-6).

AN altar is usually an elevated platform for communion with the spirit world and it is also a place of worship and sacrifice. An evil altar is the place of communion with spirits other than the Spirit of God. Many human altars can exist in our lives and we may not know it, such as self-exaltation and worship of money. Only one godly altar should stand in your life—the Lord Jesus Christ enthroned in all our hearts.

Take Away for Today

1. Are you ready to break down and smash every ungodly, evil altar that is in your life?

2. After you have exposed and destroyed the evil altars, how are you going to act and react knowing that you are His treasured possession?

A HORNET
AMONG YOUR ENEMIES

Moreover, the Lord your God will send the hornet among them until even the survivors who hide from you have perished (Deuteronomy 7:20).

NONE of your enemies will be able to hide from you. God will find them out! The hornet of God is at work on your behalf. God never ceases to amaze those who study His Word and meditate on His precepts. He is a creative God who uses various ways, people, things, animals, and even insects to fulfill His will and purpose in the world. Be alert for unusual workings of God on your behalf.

Take Away for Today

1. What do you think it means that God will send a hornet?
2. Are you hoping that God will help you battle your enemies, or are you content to let them hide from you?

OUR GOD IS THE LORD OF LORDS

For the Lord your God is God of gods and Lord of lords, the great God, mighty and awesome, who shows no partiality and accepts no bribes. He defends the cause of the fatherless and the widow, and loves the foreigner residing among you, giving them food and clothing (Deuteronomy 10:17-18).

OUR God is an awesome God! He is the Lord of lords and the King of kings. When He says yes, nobody can say no! God defends single parents, children, outcasts, and prompts us to do the same. Be encouraged today that your God will fight your battles—as He fights for those less fortunate.

Take Away for Today

1. Is there ever a time when you think God is not in control?

2. Does this Scripture passage make it clear that God is more loving, more just, and more giving than you could ever imagine?

3. Are you encouraged today knowing that God is on your side—every day in every way?

OBEDIENCE BRINGS DIVINE STRENGTH

*Observe therefore all the commands I am giving you today,
so that you may have the strength to go in and take over
the land that you are crossing the Jordan to possess, and so
that you may live long in the land that the Lord swore to
your ancestors to give to them and their descendants, a land
flowing with milk and honey* (Deuteronomy 11:8-9).

THE power and the strength of God come from obeying Him. That is why the Bible says "if you are willing and obedient you will eat the fruits of the land." We need to possess our land of milk and honey, our Promised Land. We need to take the land that He promised to our descendants rather than live in a world filled with vile leftovers. And abundant life is what He promised and what He desires for us.

Take Away for Today

1. Are you ready to live in a land flowing with milk and honey through your obedience to God?

2. Are you willing to be obedient to what the Lord says to you through His Word the Bible and when He whispers into your heart?

THE END OF HARD LABOR

The land you are entering to take over is not like the land of Egypt, from which you have come, where you planted your seed and irrigated it by foot as in a vegetable garden. But the land you are crossing the Jordan to take possession of is a land of mountains and valleys that drinks rain from heaven. It is a land the Lord your God cares for; the eyes of the Lord your God are continually on it from the beginning of the year to its end (Deuteronomy 11:10-12).

HERE the Jews were transiting from the land of hard labor to the land that drinks rain from heaven. In the past all they could afford were vegetable gardens where they "planted seed and irrigated it by foot," but soon not any more! Hardship will be over together with its misery. For many years God has cared for the land that He wants us to possess. May today be the day you accept His offer of a Promised Land and may today be the end of hard labor in your life!

Take Away for Today

1. What will it take for you to be ready to take possession of the land and life God has prepared for you to enjoy?

2. Will living a life of ease be welcomed, or will you cling to your hard labor?

Fix God's Word in Your Heart

Fix these words of mine in your hearts and minds; tie them as symbols on your hands and bind them on your foreheads. Teach them to your children, talking about them when you sit at home and when you walk along the road, when you lie down and when you get up. Write them on the doorframes of your houses and on your gates, so that your days and the days of your children may be many in the land that the Lord swore to give your forefathers, as many as the days that the heavens are above the earth (Deuteronomy 11:18-21).

HIDE the Word of God in your heart so you can obey Him under difficult and even unexpected situations. Teach His Word to your children so they can know His goodness and love. Write God's Word throughout your home—post them on your refrigerator, keep your Bibles out in plain view, play Christian music on the radio in your car, in the office, and at home. Fix God's Word in your heart and the hearts of all you know so that you may experience the days of Heaven on earth!

Take Away for Today

1. Have you fixed God's Word in your heart and mind?
2. Have you taught God's Word to your children?
3. Have you written God's Word on places where others will see and ask you about them?

LET THEM BEAR WITNESS

When the Lord your God has brought you into the land you are entering to possess, you are to proclaim on Mount Gerizim the blessings, and on Mount Ebal the curses (Deuteronomy 11:29).

FOR the Israelites this was not just a public declaration but an act of taking a stand in the presence of numerous witnesses—visible or invisible—that the Israelites were ready to play by the rules of God. It is a public show of the fairness and benevolence of the justice of God. This is a justice that is fair, balanced, and from which no one can escape. This justice is binding to the righteous or unrighteous. Like the Israelites, take a stand for God.

Take Away for Today

1. Are you ready when the time comes to be on the receiving end of God's justice?

2. Will you proclaim God's blessings after entering your Promised Land?

_____

_____

_____

A Special People

...Out of all the peoples on the face of the earth, the Lord has chosen you to be his treasured possession (Deuteronomy 14:2).

WE are a chosen generation! What a privilege. Of all the peoples of the earth, God has chosen us as His people and we are marked from other people because of His presence with us. As believers in Christ as the Son of God, we are set apart from all the other people around the world. This status should humble us as well as make us realize that we serve a great God who shows mercy to every man, woman, and child upon the face of the earth. All are welcome to join His family.

Take Away for Today

1. Do you acknowledge your specialness according to God's Word?

2. How do you honor His gift of being chosen from among all the peoples of the earth?

_____

_____

_____

WHAT A BLESSING!

Even if you have been banished to the most distant land under the heavens, from there the Lord your God will gather you and bring you back. He will bring you to the land that belonged to your ancestors, and you will take possession of it. He will make you more prosperous and numerous than your ancestors. The Lord your God will circumcise your hearts and the hearts of your descendants, so that you may love him with all your heart and with all your soul, and live. The Lord your God will put all these curses on your enemies who hate and persecute you. You will again obey the Lord and follow all his commands I am giving you today. Then the Lord your God will make you most prosperous in all the work of your hands and in the fruit of your womb, the young of your livestock and the crops of your land. The Lord will again delight in you and make you prosperous, just as he delighted in your ancestors (Deuteronomy 30:4-9).

THIS Scripture passage is full of wonderful promises from God Almighty. The living God who restores what was lost in Eden and delights in making us prosperous. What a blessing!

Take Away for Today

1. This Scripture passage is full of God's promises to those who love and obey Him. Which verse is the most meaningful to you? Why?

2. Which verse(s) is the most comforting? Why?

3. Which verse(s) is the most exciting? Why?

LIFE AND DEATH, BLESSINGS AND CURSES

This day I call heaven and earth as witnesses against you that I have set before you life and death, blessings and curses. Now choose life, so that you and your children may live and that you may love the Lord your God, listen to his voice, and hold fast to him. For the Lord is your life, and he will give you many years in the land he swore to give to your fathers, Abraham, Isaac and Jacob (Deuteronomy 30:19-20).

PRO-LIFE means standing in favor of life over death! The Scripture is clear—God is definitely pro-life! Abortion is rampant worldwide and unborn children are being tossed aside as trash; it is time for Christians to "choose life" and defend these helpless babies. We will reap rewards from God now and in heaven for taking a stand for those who are unable to defend themselves. The Lord sets decisions before us—life and death, blessings and curses. It is time we choose life and blessings!

Take Away for Today

1. Is the Lord your life? Do you feel Him weep every time one of His babies, each a miracle, is killed?

2. What do you think the toll has been on our world now that millions of children with so much potential have been murdered?

WHAT IS TRUE AND FAIR

So now you can pick out what's true and fair, find all the good trails! **Lady Wisdom** *will be your close friend, and* **Brother Knowledge** *your pleasant companion.* **Good Sense** *will* **scout** *ahead for danger,* **Insight** *will keep* **an eye** *out for you. They'll keep you from making wrong turns, or following the bad directions* (Proverbs 2:9-11 The Message).

GOD has chosen for all His children some friends to accompany us as we journey through life: Lady Wisdom, Brother Knowledge, Good Sense, and Insight. These traveling companions we should value and appreciate. As the Bible says, they will keep us from making wrong turns and following bad directions.

Take Away for Today

1. Have you asked these friends to accompany you on your daily trek toward your destiny?

2. How do you think these four companions will make a difference in your journey?

_____

_____

_____

MAY GOD BLESS YOUR SKILLS

Bless all his skills, O Lord, and be pleased with the work of his hands. Strike down those who rise up against him; strike his foes till they rise no more (Deuteronomy 33:11).

THIS is also my prayer for you today! May God establish the work of your hands and protect you from your enemies. We have been given various skills and talents to be used for God's glory. Some are plumbers, teachers, doctors, writers, engineers, care-givers, ministers—there are millions of different ways we have been gifted to bring Him glory and others relief, services, and products. We must always remember to use our talents and skills to the best of our ability.

Take Away for Today

1. Have you thanked God lately for the skills and talents He has given you?

2. Is God pleased with the work of your hands? The way you are using the skills and talents He gave you?

_____

_____

_____

WISDOM TRANSFERRED

Now Joshua son of Nun was filled with the spirit of wisdom because Moses had laid his hands on him. So the Israelites listened to him and did what the Lord had commanded Moses (Deuteronomy 34:9).

SPIRITUAL wisdom is a spirit and it is transferrable. Wisdom has a beginning because the Bible says in Proverbs that the fear of God is the beginning of wisdom. It grows in a person and can speak loudly. Today make sure you hear the voice of wisdom by listening not only with your physical ears but also with your spiritual ears and heart.

Take Away for Today

1. Have you received spiritual wisdom in response to your fear (respect) of God?
2. What is the difference between spiritual wisdom and natural wisdom?

HIS WORDS ARE LIFE

Take to heart all the words I have solemnly declared to you this day, so that you may command your children to obey carefully all the words of this law. They are not just idle words for you—they are your life (Deuteronomy 32:45-47).

THE Word of God is the power of God unto salvation, and by His Word the universe is held together. Let the Word of God be in your mouth and speak it into your situation. Rather than speaking our own words that are mostly focused on ourselves or our problems, let us take to heart the words God has written in His love letter to us—the Bible. It is wise to have a daily time apart from other activities to spend with Him and His Word.

Take Away for Today

1. Is reading and sharing the Word part of your daily routine? Your weekly routine?

2. Do you realize that His Word holds together the universe? Your country? Your job? Your family? Your life?

3. Are you giving God's Word the priority it deserves?

REMEMBER
THE GOODNESS OF THE LORD

Remember the days of old; consider the generations long past.
Ask your father and he will tell you, your elders, and they will
explain to you (Deuteronomy 32:7).

THOUGH the past is not your future, remember the *value* of the past is your testimony about how the Lord overcame on your behalf. Remember the goodness of the Lord but look forward—the past is not the future. This why God said to Moses, *"Moses my servant is dead. Now then, you and all these people, get ready to cross the Jordan River into the land I am about to give to them—to the Israelites. I will give you every place where you set your foot, as I promised Moses"* (Josh. 1:2-3).

Often the most difficult thing to put behind are the successes of yesterday that try to relive themselves as God cannot do fresh and greater things. Moses was a great man of God and no one knows that more than Joshua; but now Moses is dead, and Joshua needs to take the people to the Promised Land. The value of history is the testimony of the goodness of God—but I believe tomorrow is greater than yesterday.

Take Away for Today

1. Do you too often dwell on the past?

2. When is the last time you chose to look ahead into God's plan for your life, set goals, and then worked on a way to reach those goals?

JOIN THE COMPANY
OF GOOD PEOPLE

So—join the company of good men and women, keep your feet on the tried-and-true paths. It's the men who walk straight who will settle this land, the women with integrity who will last here. The corrupt will lose their lives; the dishonest will be gone for good (Proverbs 2:20-22 The Message).

THERE are many good men and women with whom we can choose to associate. People who walk and talk straight, telling no falsehoods and keeping their feet in respectable places. People of integrity and character who are honest and trustworthy. Yes, there are still such people in the world—seek them, befriend them, love them. For on the other side of the street resides corrupt and dishonest people who will lose their lives and be gone for good.

Take Away for Today

1. Are your friends and associates of good reputation, good company?

2. Are you of good reputation?

YOU WILL BE
PROSPEROUS AND SUCCESSFUL

*Do not let this Book of the Law depart from your mouth;
meditate on it day and night, so that you may be careful to
do everything written in it. Then you will be prosperous and
successful* (Joshua 1:8).

THE world's definition of prosperous and successful is not the
same as the Lord's definition. Although He wants us to be financially secure and have successful careers, He goes much deeper and
more substantial to include prosperity and success in our relationships, marriages, physical and spiritual health, education, emotional
well-being, and family life. He wants you to meditate on His Word so
you can live a beautiful life.

Take Away for Today

1. Do you consider yourself prosperous and successful?
2. Can you work time into your busy schedule to meditate
    on God's Word during the day and at night?

_____

_____

_____

PUT YOUR TRUST IN GOD

Have I not commanded you? Be strong and courageous. Do not be terrified; do not be discouraged, for the Lord your God will be with you wherever you go (Joshua 1:9).

PUT your trust in no person, let your trust be in the Lord. He will never fail. When you awake in the morning, God is beside you, ready to start your day. When you go about your daily tasks, Jesus is walking along beside you, ready and willing to guide you. When you lay your head down at night, the Holy Spirit lays with you, ready to bring you a peaceful and restful sleep. There is no need to be terrified or discouraged—your God is with you.

Take Away for Today

1. Has this verse brought peace to your heart?
2. Is this verse important enough to write it on your heart? Post it on your refrigerator? Keep it in your wallet?

_____

_____

_____

HIS WAYS ARE NOT OUR WAYS

Then the Lord said to Joshua, "See, I have delivered Jericho into your hands, along with its king and its fighting men. March around the city once with all the armed men. Do this for six days. Have seven priests carry trumpets of rams' horns in front of the ark. On the seventh day, march around the city seven times, with the priests blowing the trumpets. When you hear them sound a long blast on the trumpets, have the whole army give a loud shout; then the wall of the city will collapse and the army will go up, everyone straight in" (Joshua 6:2-5).

THE Lord told Joshua exactly how to conquer and possess the city of Jericho. The Lord told Noah exactly how to build the ark to save the animals and his family. If we listen closely enough, the Lord will tell us exactly how to possess what we need and how to save the innocent. His ways may sound strange, but we must obey.

Take Away for Today

1. How willing are you to do strange things because God has asked you to do so?

2. If you were Joshua or Noah, do you think you would have obeyed the Lord's odd instructions?

ACHAN'S SIN

But keep away from the devoted things, so that you will not bring about your own destruction by taking any of them. Otherwise you will make the camp of Israel liable to destruction and bring trouble on it. All the silver and gold and the articles of bronze and iron are sacred to the Lord and must go into his treasury. ...But the Israelites were unfaithful in regard to the devoted things; Achan son of Karmi, the son of Zimri, the son of Zerah, of the tribe of Judah, took some of them. So the Lord's anger burned against Israel (Joshua 6:18-19; 7:1).

ACHAN went directly against what the Lord commanded. Rather than keeping away from idols and things devoted to other gods, he took some of them and brought them into the midst of the Israelites. The Lord was burning angry. Achan's greed was more powerful than his devotion to God. This must not be true of us. A greedy nature must be squashed immediately upon discovery.

Take Away for Today

1. Are you aware when greed slips into your mind? Do you quickly rid yourself of it?

2. Has greed ever overpowered your sensibilities and made you do something you regretted later?

YOU HAVE SINNED, BUT...

*The Lord said to Joshua, "Stand up! What are you doing down on your face? **Israel has sinned;** they have violated my covenant, which I commanded them to keep. **They have taken some of the devoted things; they have stolen, they have lied, they have put them with their own possessions.** That is why the Israelites cannot stand against their enemies; they turn their backs and run because they have been made liable to destruction. **I will not be with you anymore unless you destroy whatever among you is devoted to destruction*** (Joshua 7:10-12).*

THE Lord was angry with the people for stealing and lying and bringing destruction within. We must always be aware of what we bring into our midst. We may be bringing destruction upon ourselves by disregarding His covenant with us. We must be willing to destroy whatever is keeping us from being one with Christ.

Take Away for Today

1. Although you sin, what remedy do you have to be restored into His arms?

2. Have you stolen or lied and brought something not devoted to God into your life?

THE BATTLE BELONGS TO THE LORD

After an all-night march from Gilgal, Joshua took them by surprise. The Lord threw them into confusion before Israel, so Joshua and the Israelites defeated them completely at Gibeon. Israel pursued them along the road going up to Beth Horon and cut them down all the way to Azekah and Makkedah. As they fled before Israel on the road down from Beth Horon to Azekah, the Lord hurled large hailstones down on them, and more of them died from the hail than were killed by the swords of the Israelites (Joshua 10:9-11).

JOSHUA and his men had the enemy on the run because the Lord was with them and confused the enemy. As the enemy was running away God pelted them with hailstones that killed more of them than Joshua's men's swords. The battle truly belonged the Lord. He will fight our battles for us—if we give Him permission, if we obey Him, if we trust Him.

Take Away for Today

1. Why do you think God used hailstones to defeat the enemy? Why not lightning or another act of nature?

2. Do you think God uses acts of nature to defeat today's enemies?

THE BULLY

Don't walk around with a chip on your shoulder, always spoiling for a fight. Don't try to be like those who shoulder their way through life. Why be a bully? "Why not?" you say. Because God can't stand twisted souls. It's the straightforward who get his respect (Proverbs 3:30-32 The Message).

NO one likes a bully. The only friends a bully has are those who are so intimidated that they can't refuse his or her requests for a so-called friendship. We need to be careful of appearing to have a chip on our shoulder, being antagonistic and quarrelsome. These are not personality traits that fit with the Kingdom lifestyle.

Take Away for Today

1. What does the phrase mean to you, "who shoulder their way through life"?

2. How about the phrase "twisted souls"?

A SET UP?

...But Samson said to his father, "Get her for me. She's the right one for me." (His parents did not know that this was from the Lord, who was seeking an occasion to confront the Philistines; for at that time they were ruling over Israel.)
(Judges 14:3-4).

SAMSON insisted on marrying a woman not from his own people. She was a Philistine, from the uncircumcised people. He persuaded his parents to "get her" for him. Although this went against what his parents believed to be right, Samson was united with this woman. But was this entire event a set up by God *"who was seeking an occasion to confront the Philistines"*?

Take Away for Today

1. Does God set up events to get His own way?
2. Has God set up events in your life? How have they worked out?

THE SPIRIT OF GOD CAN CHANGE A PERSON

After that you will go to Gibeah of God, where there is a Philistine outpost. As you approach the town, you will meet a procession of prophets coming down from the high place with lyres, tambourines, flutes and harps being played before them, and they will be prophesying. The Spirit of the Lord will come upon you in power, and you will prophesy with them; and you will be changed into a different person. Once these signs are fulfilled, do whatever your hand finds to do, for God is with you (1 Samuel 10:5-7).

SAMUEL was talking to Saul in this passage from First Samuel. Samuel told Saul that God was with him and that he would be a changed person after the encounter. The Lord was going to come upon Saul with power and he would prophesy. No doubt Saul was confused and amazed at what he heard from Samuel. It is true that we will be changed into a different person after the Spirit of the Lord comes upon us. We should welcome these times and accept the change graciously and thankfully.

Take Away for Today

1. Are you a different person now that you are a believer in Christ, God's Son?

2. In what ways are you different from the person you used to be?

RUN TO GOD!

Trust God from the bottom of your heart; don't try to figure out everything on your own. Listen for God's voice in everything you do, everywhere you go; he's the one who will keep you on track. Don't assume that you know it all. Run to God! Run from evil! (Proverbs 3:5-7 The Message)

CASUALLY trusting God as we trust that gravity will keep us sitting in our chair is not the same trust we are told to have in God. We are to "Trust God from the bottom of [our] hearts"! That's a deep and abiding trust that belongs only to our heavenly Father. And we are to listen for God's voice in everything we do and everywhere we go! And we must "Run to God!"—not walk nonchalantly, run! This passage in Proverbs puts our action into high gear. Let's do it!

Take Away for Today

1. Are you ready to switch into high gear and run to God and away from evil?

2. Will you stop trying to figure out everything on your own and assuming that you know it all?

_____

_____

_____

EVIL GROPES

And now, behold, the hand of the Lord is upon you, and you will be blind, [so blind that you will be] unable to see the sun for a time. Instantly there fell upon him a mist and a darkness, and he groped about seeking persons who would lead him by the hand (Acts 13:11 AMP).

ELYMAS, the evil son of the devil, was struck blind by the Lord. He was stopped in his tracks by the hand of the Lord, just as Paul said. Therefore, the evil one's tactics were halted and the Lord was once again in control. Evil could no longer lead people into the wrong ways, along the wrong path. Now evil was groping around trying to find someone to lead him! Let God arise and let his enemy be confused and scattered. Groping in darkness is the eventual fate of all the enemies of God!

Take Away for Today

1. You have the power to blind the enemy, the evil in your life. Are you using that power?

2. Are you groping in the dark to find someone to lead you…or are you holding on to the Light of life walking safely and securely into your destiny?

EVERY BLESSING IN CHRIST

Praise be to the God and Father of our Lord Jesus Christ, who has blessed us in the heavenly realms with every spiritual blessing in Christ (Ephesians 1:3).

THERE is an incredible truth in this Scripture verse—we have every blessing in Christ. All that is required of us is to work those blessings into the realities of our lives. Every day there are ways to use the blessings we have to help others, increase our productivity, motivate us, and shine a light on the One who provides the blessings.

Every blessing has duality of existence; it always exists in the heavenly realm and when we satisfy the conditions for it to manifest in the natural realm, then we have it. Work the blessings waiting for you in the heavenly realm into your physical life.

Take Away for Today

1.   What spiritual blessings are you most thankful for?
2.   How have you worked God's blessings into your life? Your family? Your workplace?

CONFORMING WITH THE PURPOSE OF HIS WILL

In him we were also chosen, having been predestined according to the plan of him who works out everything in conformity with the purpose of his will (Ephesians 1:11).

GOD is working out everything to conform with the purpose of His will. We are not born with the perfect attitude, lifestyle, or mindset. We must conform to the Kingdom way of thinking and living. Conformity doesn't mean we have to leave behind our own personality and uniqueness. On the contrary, we have been divinely designed for greatness in our own way. Conforming means to obey His commands for our lives, which are only ever to bring out the best within us.

Take Away for Today

1. How does being predestined according to His plan fit in with choosing to follow Him?

2. Did God choose you or did you choose God?

THE SPIRIT OF WISDOM AND REVELATION

I keep asking that the God of our Lord Jesus Christ, the glorious Father, may give you the Spirit of wisdom and revelation, so that you may know him better. I pray that the eyes of your heart may be enlightened in order that you may know the hope to which he has called you, the riches of his glorious inheritance in his holy people, and his incomparably great power for us who believe... (Ephesians 1:17-19).

THE more we get to know our heavenly Father, the more our heart will be enlightened. Enlightenment through Jesus Christ means we have hope in attaining all of the riches He has promised. We can gratefully accept our glorious inheritance with the Spirit of wisdom and revelation—just as He planned for us to do from before we were born.

Take Away for Today

1. Do you ask God to fill you with the Spirit of wisdom and revelation?

2. What do you think this Spirit will do for you? How will it make a difference in your life? In your perspective?

GOD'S ABSOLUTE POWER AND AUTHORITY

far above all rule and authority, power and dominion, and
every name that is invoked, not only in the present age but
also in the one to come. And God placed all things under
his feet and appointed him to be head over everything for
the church, which is his body, the fullness of him who fills
everything in every way (Ephesians 1:21-23).

WHEN we face pressure from the devil and his evil cohorts, many forget that all power belongs to God—the Alpha and Omega, and Creator of the universe, the visible and invisible. God is the head; He has always been the head of the church, His creation, the entire universe. He is the beginning and the end. On the other hand, it is also unwise to put church leaders, pastors, or healers above God the Almighty. We must be cautious when humans rise to a status that is too high, too easy for people to confuse God with what is not God. Remember, the devil is not competing and equal to God in any way, but in every way remains under God!

Take Away for Today

1. Do you hold only God as the absolute power and authority in your life?

2. Have you witnessed ministry leaders who hold themselves higher than others, almost or as high as God Himself?

_____

_____

GLOWING WITH HEALTH

Your body will glow with health, your very bones will vibrate with life! Honor God with everything you own; give him the first and the best (Proverbs 3:8-9 The Message).

ISN'T that a great verse, "Your body will glow with health, your very bones will vibrate with life!"? When our bodies are healthy our minds are usually clear and our outlook optimistic. That great verse is followed by a command that will bring about good health, "Honor God with everything you own; give Him the first and the best." This is the least we can do in exchange for all He has done for us, right?

Take Away for Today

1. Can you think of a better way to describe a healthy body?

2. Can you think of a better way to repay God for all His love?

GOD'S INTENT

His intent was that now, through the church, the manifold wisdom of God should be made known to the rulers and authorities in the heavenly realms, according to his eternal purpose that he accomplished in Christ Jesus our Lord (Ephesians 3:10-11).

GOD'S intent is to make known His manifold wisdom to ministers and leaders according to His good and perfect will. As such we should respect them and listen to what God has given them to share with His people. Church leaders have an important responsibility and an eternal purpose to carry out the plan set into motion by the sacrifice of Christ Jesus, our Lord and Savior.

Take Away for Today

1. Do you pray for your ministry and church leaders?
2. How serious do you take the role of church leader?
3. Do you give your church leader the respect he or she deserves?

DO NOT DEPART FROM THE TRUE GOSPEL

But even if we or an angel from heaven should preach a gospel other than the one we preached to you, let them be under God's curse! (Galatians 1:8)

PREACHING and teaching the true gospel is vital. According to what Paul wrote to the Galatians, if a person—or even an angel from heaven—preaches anything other than the true gospel that person will be under God's curse! That is a powerful and frightening statement that Paul made. So it would benefit us to seek God's face before preaching or teaching, always vigilant that His Word is the only word coming from our mouths.

Take Away for Today

1. How can you be sure you are speaking the true gospel?
2. What is the true gospel? Write your definition.

_____

_____

_____

ZEALOUS FOR THE WRONG REASON

I was advancing in Judaism beyond many of my own age among my people and was extremely zealous for the traditions of my fathers. But when God, who set me apart from my mother's womb and called me by his grace, was pleased to reveal his Son in me so that I might preach him among the Gentiles... (Galatians 1:14-16).

MANY people in many religions are zealous—defined as "marked by a fervent partisanship for a person, a cause, or an ideal; intense, passionate, ardently active." Throughout the centuries, wars were fought in zealous rage to spread certain beliefs and philosophies. Today we hear of some being "radical" in their zealousness to impose their beliefs unto others. May we be zealous for the right reasons—the reasons of love, respect, and righteousness in the saving grace of our Lord; indeed as Paul said, *"against such there is no law"* (Gal. 5:23).

Take Away for Today

1. Have you ever been approached by a zealous person of another faith?

2. How did you react to that person?

NO LONGER ME, BUT CHRIST

For through the law I died to the law so that I might live for God. I have been crucified with Christ and I no longer live, but Christ lives in me. The life I now live in the body, I live by faith in the Son of God, who loved me and gave himself for me. I do not set aside the grace of God, for if righteousness could be gained through the law, Christ died for nothing!
(Galatians 2:19-21)

PAUL became such a different person when he accepted the Lord as his Savior that his name was changed from Saul to Paul. The Amplified version says, *"I have been crucified with Christ [in Him I have shared His crucifixion]; it is no longer I who live, but Christ (the Messiah) lives in me; and the life I now live in the body **I live by faith in (by adherence to and reliance on and complete trust in) the Son of God, Who loved me and gave Himself up for me."** This was total transformation for Paul and it should be for us all as well.

Take Away for Today

1. Have you been totally transformed by the saving grace of God?

2. Do you live by faith?

SMART AND STUPID

*God won't starve an honest soul, but he frustrates the appetites
of the wicked. Sloth makes you poor; diligence brings wealth.
Make hay while the sun shines—that's smart; go fishing during
harvest—that's stupid (Proverbs 3-5 The Message).*

B ECAUSE we are honest souls, God will provide nourishment for
us. And He says that being lazy will make us poor, but diligent
work brings us wealth. We are to "Make hay while the sun shines,"
which is a smart thing to do. But going fishing when we should be
at home harvesting—that's stupid. The passage may be stating the
obvious, but in these times, what used to be obvious isn't always so.

Take Away for Today

1. As an honest soul, are you being fed and enjoying wealth?

2. Are you making hay while the sun is shining? In other
   words, are you taking advantage of the opportunities
   that God is setting before you?

ABRAHAM IS YOUR FATHER

Understand, then, that those who have faith are children of Abraham. Scripture foresaw that God would justify the Gentiles by faith, and announced the gospel in advance to Abraham: "All nations will be blessed through you." So those who rely on faith are blessed along with Abraham, the man of faith (Galatians 3:7-9).

ACCORDING this this Scripture passage, Abraham is our spiritual father. God blessed all the nations through Abraham. Looking at the world today, many nations don't recognize Abraham as their spiritual father—he is just another biblical character in ancient days gone by. As "the man of faith," we have a lot to learn from Abraham.

Take Away for Today

1. How seriously do you take the fact that Abraham is your spiritual father?

2. How well do you know the life of Abraham? Is it worth time to study him?

3. How special was Abraham's relationship with God?

ONE IN CHRIST

So in Christ Jesus you are all children of God through faith, for all of you who were baptized into Christ have clothed yourselves with Christ. There is neither Jew nor Gentile, neither slave nor free, nor is there male and female, for you are all one in Christ Jesus. If you belong to Christ, then you are Abraham's seed, and heirs according to the promise (Galatians 3:26-29).

P AUL mentions again that we are all "Abraham's seed," which makes us heirs to the Kingdom of God. As children of God through faith, all of humankind is linked together. He sees every human being as His creation, brought into the world by the miracle of physical birth and brought into His Kingdom by the miracle of spiritual birth. His desire that all will come to know Him—and that none would perish. As the Bible says, *"From one man he made all the nations, that they should inhabit the whole earth; and he marked out their appointed times in history and the boundaries of their lands. God did this so that they would seek him and perhaps reach out for him and find him, though he is not far from any one of us. 'For in him we live and move and have our being.' As some of your own poets have said, 'We are his offspring'"* (Acts 17:26-28).

Take Away for Today

1. Do you consider yourself a brother or sister to the homeless person on the corner? The Hindu Sikh down the street? The radical Muslim across town?

2. Have you been "baptized into Christ" and "clothed with Christ"?

THE SET TIME IS NOW

But when the time arrived that was set by God the Father, God sent his Son, born among us of a woman, born under the conditions of the law so that he might redeem those of us who have been kidnapped by the law. Thus we have been set free to experience our rightful heritage. You can tell for sure that you are now fully adopted as his own children because God sent the Spirit of his Son into our lives crying out, "Papa! Father!" Doesn't that privilege of intimate conversation with God make it plain that you are not a slave, but a child? And if you are a child, you're also an heir, with complete access to the inheritance (Galatians 4:4-7 The Message).

R ATHER than being kidnapped by the law, we are now set free to enjoy our inheritance in Christ, in His Kingdom of abundant life. God's timing is always perfect. He is in control of time and uses it to His advantage and our benefit. Therefore we can come before Him as a beloved child, nestling next to Him and talking to each other as Father and child. This is what Jesus, our Brother, did for us at the cross.

Take Away for Today

1. Have you ever cried out "Papa, Father," knowing that He is close enough to allow you to be so intimate in your calling?

2. How is spiritual adoption by God different from natural birth by your natural parents?

PROCESS PAINS

My dear children, for whom I am again in the pains of
childbirth until Christ is formed in you (Galatians 4:19).

EXPERIENCING spiritual birth may involve some pain. But the pain is short-lived and the result is eternal life. You may experience the pain of giving up your unhealthy lifestyle, your bad temper, your habit that will cause cancer, your tendency to be lazy. The pain you experience will be quickly followed by the knowledge that you have gained freedom and have been set free from all the things holding you back from living an exciting and healthy life.

Take Away for Today

1. How willing are you to experience short-term pain to gain long-term joy?

2. A life of joy and peace is awaiting you—are you ready to live it?

SET FREE FOR FREEDOM

It is for freedom that Christ has set us free. Stand firm, then, and do not let yourselves be burdened again by a yoke of slavery (Galatians 5:1).

CHRIST has set us free to live a good life—a life filled with victory. We need to stand strong in this knowledge and not allow the evil one or our selfish desires to chain us up. We need to realize the cage that sin puts us in and determine to live free, unharnessed.

Take Away for Today

1. Are you truly free?
2. Is there an area in your life where you feel chained, unable to free yourself?
3. What is holding you back from giving this area over to Christ who can and will set you free?

_____

_____

_____

WHO CUT IN ON YOU?

You were running superbly! Who cut in on you, deflecting you from the true course of obedience? This detour doesn't come from the One who called you into the race in the first place. And please don't toss this off as insignificant. It only takes a minute amount of yeast, you know, to permeate an entire loaf of bread. Deep down, the Master has given me confidence that you will not defect. But the one who is upsetting you, whoever he is, will bear the divine judgment (Galatians 5:7-10 The Message).

WHEN going along in life and doing the best we can, sometimes someone or something cuts into our lives and causes us to detour from our true course. It is important that we stay on the path that God set before us. We can't afford to be pushed off the right and true way because the lion is ready and waiting to devour us if we do (see 1 Pet. 5:8). Paul was surprised at the Galatians and he said, *"You were running superbly! Who cut in on you..."* Don't allow anything to derail you from following God and His ways.

Take Away for Today

1. Have you been shoved off course and you are now on a different path from the one God intended for you?

2. What can you do to get back on the right course?

ACTS OF THE FLESH

The acts of the flesh are obvious: sexual immorality, impurity and debauchery; idolatry and witchcraft; hatred, discord, jealousy, fits of rage, selfish ambition, dissensions, factions and envy; drunkenness, orgies, and the like. I warn you, as I did before, that those who live like this will not inherit the kingdom of God (Galatians 5:19-21).

SOMETIMES we are knocked off course by acts of the flesh. The evil one knows how tempting these acts are—how they reach into the bottom layer of ourselves to dig out the worst in us. If we want to inherit the Kingdom of God, we must, absolutely, stay away from all of the sins mentioned in this Scripture passage. God will give us the strength and the encouragement we need to stay away from these acts of the flesh. Ask Him; He will provide.

Take Away for Today

1. Have you been tempted by these snares of the evil one?
2. How can you be assured of not falling into sin or giving in to these acts of the flesh?

LIVE BY THE SPIRIT

Brothers and sisters, if someone is caught in a sin, you who live by the Spirit should restore that person gently. But watch yourselves, or you also may be tempted. If anyone thinks they are something when they are not, they deceive themselves. Each one should test their own actions. Do not be deceived: God cannot be mocked. A man reaps what he sows. Whoever sows to please their flesh, from the flesh will reap destruction; whoever sows to please the Spirit, from the Spirit will reap eternal life (Galatians 6:1,3-4,7-8).

WE reap what we sow. What goes around comes around. These are familiar phrases because they have been proven correct many times over many years by many people. When we sow seeds of honor and respect, we will receive such in return. If we go around gossiping and back biting, those words will come back to haunt us. Let us rather live by the Spirit who is truth, justice, and love.

Take Away for Today

1. In your experience, have these phrases been proven true?
2. Are you going to be pleased or unhappy when what you have been sending around comes back to you?

AT THE PROPER TIME

*Let us not become weary in doing good, for at the proper time
we will reap a harvest if we do not give up. Therefore, as we
have opportunity, let us do good to all people, especially to
those who belong to the family of believers. May I never boast
except in the cross of our Lord Jesus Christ, through which the
world has been crucified to me, and I to the world. Neither
circumcision nor uncircumcision means anything; what
counts is the new creation (Galatians 6:9-10,14-15).*

AS mentioned previously, God's timing is perfect and this we
must remember as we live by the Spirit in accordance with His
Word. As opportunities arise for us to do good to others, especially
other believers, let us not mumble and grumble but rather lend a
helping hand—for that is what Jesus did for us while we were still
sinners (see Rom. 5:8). Don't give up; your reward is near if you don't
give up and if you wait patiently for the proper time. There is a divine
time for everything under the sun. God makes everything beautiful
in its time.

Take Away for Today

1. Do you sometimes get tired of being tired?
2. Do you sometimes forget to call on the Lord so He can
   give you rest and peace?

TRUE INTENTIONS
WILL BE REVEALED

Other Benjaminites and some men from Judah also came to David in his stronghold. David went out to meet them and said to them, "If you have come to me in peace to help me, I am ready for you to join me. But if you have come to betray me to my enemies when my hands are free from violence, may the God of our ancestors see it and judge you (1 Chronicles 12:16-17).

A T times it is hard to tell a person's true intentions and motivations. When David was building his army, men came to him who were unknown. Rather than guessing or worrying about their intentions, he confronted them directly. In the same way, if you are uncomfortable or have a nagging suspicion about people, ask them directly about their intentions. Welcome them if what you hear bears witness with your spirit. Dismiss them if what you hear is contrary to the Word of God. But our God will reveal the hidden intentions of others.

Take Away for Today

1. Have you had suspicions about someone but were unsure about how to handle the situation?

2. Have you welcomed new people into your life who have declared their honorable intentions?

_____

_____

_____

THOUGH THEY CELEBRATED, GOD WAS GRIEVED

They moved the ark of God from Abinadab's house on a new cart, with Uzzah and Ahio guiding it. David and all the Israelites were celebrating with all their might before God, with songs and with harps, lyres, timbrels, cymbals and trumpets (1 Chronicles 13:7-8).

DAVID and the Israelites were in presumption; they carried the ark in new cart, but that was not the way God prescribed for carrying the ark. Because of the irreverent act bounding on disobedience, God was grieved, their celebrations and excitements notwithstanding. It is important not only to do good things but to do them in a godly way. Let your actions line up with the will of God.

Take Away for Today

1. Do you sometimes rush ahead and take action before asking God for direction?
2. Are you careful to do good things in a godly way?

_____

_____

_____

OKAY UNTIL THE TESTING

When they came to the threshing floor of Kidon, Uzzah reached out his hand to steady the ark, because the oxen stumbled. The Lord's anger burned against Uzzah, and he struck him down because he had put his hand on the ark. So he died there before God (1 Chronicles 13:9-10).

W E must make sure our actions are rooted in the solid foundation of the will of God as enunciated in His Word. If not, while things may look okay on the surface and run smoothly, when testing comes, the truth will be revealed and what is hidden will be exposed in times of trial. The oxen instead of the shoulder of the Levite can carry the ark, but when the oxen stumbled, the hidden error was manifested.

The truth will be revealed in times of trial.

Take Away for Today

1. Although there may be a way that seems right, it is imperative to ask God which is His way. Do you agree based on the Scripture?

2. In times of trial, are hidden motivations exposed so you can make corrections?

THE BLESSING OF OBED-EDOM

He did not take the ark to be with him in the City of David. Instead, he took it to the house of Obed-Edom the Gittite. The ark of God remained with the family of Obed-Edom in his house for three months, and the Lord blessed his household and everything he had (1 Chronicles 13:13-14).

GOD blesses all the household where He is welcomed. When the ark was in the home of Obed-Edom, the family and "everything he had" was blessed. We can be assured of blessings when we welcome the Lord into our homes and hearts. *"I do all this for the sake of the gospel, that I may share in its blessings"* (1 Cor. 9:23).

Take Away for Today

1. Do you welcome the Lord into your home and heart on a daily basis?

2. In what ways do you think the family of Obed-Edom was blessed?

DON'T ALLOW UNGODLINESS
TO SNEAK IN

So David and his men went up to Baal Perazim, and there he defeated them. He said, "As waters break out, God has broken out against my enemies by my hand." So that place was called Baal Perazim. The Philistines had abandoned their gods there, and David gave orders to burn them in the fire (1 Chronicles 14:11-12).

EVEN in the time of great breakthrough mentioned above, ungodliness wanted to subtly sneak in. In modern times there are many blessings, but we should watch for any consequential ungodliness that may hide around the corner. The Internet is a great blessing, but it has many attendant ungodly aspects that can spiritually cripple unsuspecting people. When false gods, idols, and anything that is ungodly enters our lives or our homes, we must be diligent about destroying them as soon as we realize their existence. Sometimes the evil one is subtle about introducing ungodly things or persons into our lives, so we must pay close attention to our surroundings.

Take Away for Today

1. Has something ungodly slipped into your home or work life that you need to destroy?
2. Has your home been invaded by ungodly music, video games, television shows?

EVERY DAY NEEDS A FRESH MANDATE

Once more the Philistines raided the valley; so David inquired of God again, and God answered him, "Do not go directly after them, but circle around them and attack them in front of the poplar trees. As soon as you hear the sound of marching in the tops of the poplar trees, move out to battle, because that will mean God has gone out in front of you to strike the Philistine army." So David did as God commanded him, and they struck down the Philistine army, all the way from Gibeon to Gezer (1 Chronicles 14:13-16).

ALTHOUGH we may have sought God for His direction yesterday, as David did, we should continue to seek His direction daily. Only He knows the future, the beginning to the end, so seeking His guidance consistently is the key to continuing in the right pathway. Asking Him assures us that He has gone out in front of us to clear the way.

Take Away for Today

1. Are you seeking a fresh mandate daily from God?
2. Are you convinced that God is out in front of you, clearing the way for you to advance toward your God-given destiny?

BLESSINGS ACCRUE

*Blessings accrue on a good and honest life, but the mouth of
the wicked is a dark cave of abuse. A good and honest life is
a blessed memorial; a wicked life leaves a rotten stench. A
wise heart takes orders; an empty head will come unglued.
Honesty lives confident and carefree, but Shifty is sure to be
exposed (Proverbs 10:6-9 The Message).*

PROVERBS is full of good advice from the Lord. If we just took
one a day, meditated on it and then put the advice to work for us,
we would be very happy Christians indeed. The metaphors within
this passage are worthy of serious contemplation. After all, we must
consider the good with the bad—and choose the good! May blessings
accrue as you live a good and honest life!

Take Away for Today

1. Have you ever experienced someone whose wicked
   mouth was a dark cave of abuse?

2. Because you have an honest and wise heart, are you
   agreeable to taking orders and living confident and
   carefree?

DAVID RETURNED TO BLESS HIS HOUSEHOLD

Then all the people left, each for their own home, and David returned home to bless his family (1 Chronicles 16:43).

LEADERS such as David have enormous responsibilities that often keep them away from their families and homes. After fulfilling their responsibilities that involve (and bless) many people, even nations, they must remember to *return home and bless* their individual families as well. Families are the glue that hold societies together—that hold people accountable to each other. Let's not forget to bless our individual family members, giving hugs for achievements and encouragement for striving.

Take Away for Today

1. Do you bless your spouse and your children regularly? In what ways?
2. Are you a blessing to those around you by sharing smiles, a kind word, and the like?

ARMY OF GIANT KILLERS

In another battle with the Philistines, Elhanan son of Jair killed Lahmi the brother of Goliath the Gittite, who had a spear with a shaft like a weaver's rod. In still another battle, which took place at Gath, there was a huge man with six fingers on each hand and six toes on each foot—twenty-four in all. He also was descended from Rapha. When he taunted Israel, Jonathan son of Shimea, David's brother, killed him (1 Chronicles 20:5-7).

THE Philistines warred with the Israelites on numerous occasions. Each time it seemed there was an oddity about—the giant Goliath, the "huge man with six fingers on each hand and six toes on each foot, for examples. When Israel called on God Almighty to battle for them, it mattered not the oddity or the statue of the soldiers, God toppled the giants. No matter what the odd giant is in your life, God is willing and able to destroy it. Elhanan, Jonathan and David were giant killers and they are from one army—the army of giant killers—David's army which was like the "army of God." You belong to the army of giant killers!

Take Away for Today

1. Are you distracted by odd occurrences in your life, so much so that you are afraid to call on the Almighty Warrior to step in and fight for you?

2. Is the enemy taunting you? Have you called in your "Secret Weapon" to help?

_____

_____

LET ME FALL INTO THE HANDS OF THE LORD

David said to Gad, "I am in deep distress. Let me fall into the hands of the Lord, for his mercy is very great; but do not let me fall into human hands" (1 Chronicles 21:13).

DAVID was a man after God's own heart, so he knew how merciful God is. We should know this is true as well because God sent His only Son to earth to live and die and be raised from the dead—all for us, all through His merciful heart. When we "fall into the hands of the Lord," we know we will be treated justly. The same cannot be said of "falling into human hands."

Take Away for Today

1. Would you rather be judged by God or by humans?
2. What do you think the verdict would be if you were to be charged with being a Christian? Is there enough evidence to convict you?

GOD IS FULL OF MERCY

And God sent an angel to destroy Jerusalem. But as the angel was doing so, the Lord saw it and relented concerning the disaster and said to the angel who was destroying the people, "Enough! Withdraw your hand." The angel of the Lord was then standing at the threshing floor of Araunah the Jebusite. David looked up and saw the angel of the Lord standing between heaven and earth, with a drawn sword in his hand extended over Jerusalem (1 Chronicles 21:16).

E VEN though God had just cause to send an angel to destroy Jerusalem, at the last moment God told the angel to stop. God has control over angels, demons, life, death, and over all of His creation. God is a fair and just God who sent His Son as the ultimate sign of His infinite mercy toward His pitiful and sinful children. Let us this day and every day be thankful for His mercy. Today I say "ENOUGH!" to the reoccurring work of punishment in your life and family, for His mercy is the exception from punishment.

Take Away for Today

1. Why do you think God told the angel to put away his sword that he had extended over Jerusalem?

2. David saw the angel of the Lord standing between heaven and earth. What do you think about that scene?

Reading the Bible in a Year: Proverbs 3-4 and 1 Corinthians 13.

THE VALUE AND COST OF SACRIFICE

David said to him, "Let me have the site of your threshing floor so I can build an altar to the Lord, that the plague on the people may be stopped. Sell it to me at the full price." Araunah said to David, "Take it! Let my lord the king do whatever pleases him. Look, I will give...the threshing sledges for the wood, and the wheat for the grain offering. I will give all this." But King David replied to Araunah, "No, I insist on paying the full price. I will not take for the Lord what is yours, or sacrifice a burnt offering that costs me nothing" (1 Chronicles 21:24).

SACRIFICE is not sacrifice if it costs us nothing. Sacrifice comes at a cost. King David knew this and was willing to pay. Jesus sacrificed His life for us. We must be willing to pay the cost of sacrificing ourselves as an offering to the Lord. If that means we sacrifice sleep to meditate on the Word or getting up early to attend church, then we should be willing to do so. None of our sacrifices will ever be in vain. Remember, God loves and rewards cheerful givers. The value of a sacrifice is often measured by the cost of the sacrifice!

Take Away for Today

1. Are you willing to pay the cost of being a child of God?
2. What have you sacrificed lately for the Lord?

ARAUNAH'S THRESHING FLOOR

Then the Lord spoke to the angel, and he put his sword back into its sheath. At that time, when David saw that the Lord had answered him on the threshing floor of Araunah the Jebusite, he offered sacrifices there. The tabernacle of the Lord, which Moses had made in the wilderness, and the altar of burnt offering were at that time on the high place at Gibeon. But David could not go before it to inquire of God, because he was afraid of the sword of the angel of the Lord. ...Then David said, "The house of the Lord God is to be here, and also the altar of burnt offering for Israel" (1 Chronicles 21:27-30; 22:1).

A RAUNAH'S threshing floor is renowned for many reasons; it's the place of sacrifice, for it is the place where Abraham attempted to sacrifice Isaac. Instead God provided a lamb ready for sacrifice; it is therefore a place of divine provision. It is also a threshing floor, a place for travailing in prayers. It is the place King Solomon chose for the Temple of the Lord, a place of worship; and it is currently the place where the Islamic shrine is located, the well-known Dome of Rock. It is a place highly contested for by godly and ungodly spirits. From the Scripture above, it is also a place of mercy, where God had mercy on His people.

No matter where you are today, let it be your altar for God—it can be your threshing floor; like David built an altar and presented offerings to God. Whenever you are driving to work, sitting on a bus, shopping for groceries, you can connect with God and offer Him your thanksgiving and praise for His holiness.

Take Away for Today

1. Where is your favorite "threshing floor" to present your sacrifices to God?

2. If you could build a special place where you could go to be with God, where would it be and what would it look like?

_____

_____

_____

DAVID'S PREPARATIONS

David said, "My son Solomon is young and inexperienced, and the house to be built for the Lord should be of great magnificence and fame and splendor in the sight of all the nations. Therefore I will make preparations for it." So David made extensive preparations before his death (1 Chronicles 22:5).

PARENTS know their children intimately. David knew he would not live long enough to see the Temple built, so he looked ahead and made preparations so that his son Solomon could complete the project. Rather than becoming depressed and despondent about his approaching death, David chose to look ahead, make plans, and offer very valuable assistance to his son. For their tomorrow, let us make sacrifices from our today!

Take Away for Today

1. Are you looking ahead, making plans, and assisting others?
2. Have you allowed an upsetting doctor's report or an illness turn you inward rather than toward the Lord?

BREAKING THE SPIRIT OF OFFENSE

We give no offense in anything, that our ministry may not be blamed (2 Corinthians 6:3 NKJV).

O FFENSE is like a cancan worm eating from within. Therefore let this be your desire; that you will refuse to be offended, or to offend. Like Paul says, *"give no offense in anything"*; *"either to Jews or to the Greeks"* (1 Cor. 10:32 NKJV). That you will *"always strive to have a conscience without offense"* (Acts 24:16 NKJV). This is the sure way to ensure that every morning you will hear the refreshing wind of the Holy Spirit in your life as you welcome Him into your place. May the blood of Jesus break the power of offense over your life.

Take Away for Today

1. Are you easily offended? Why?
2. Do you often offend? Why?
3. Write in your own words, including your current or a past situation, First Corinthians 10:32 and Acts 24:16.

CLEANSING AND WASHING

*Therefore, brothers, since we have confidence to enter the Most Holy Place by the blood of Jesus, by a new and living way opened for us through the curtain, that is, his body, and since we have a great priest over the house of God, **let us draw near to God with a sincere heart in full assurance of faith, having our hearts sprinkled to cleanse us from a guilty conscience and having our bodies washed with pure water*** (Hebrews 10:19-22).

ALL people are born with a sinful nature. To destroy that nature, we must be born again. We must draw near to God with sincere hearts and full of faith. That way we can be rid of a guilty conscience and our bodies can be washed clean with the pure water that flows from our heavenly Father.

Take Away for Today

1. What is the easiest way to cleanse a guilty conscience?
2. Have you ever washed your body with dirty water? What would be the point?

VENGEANCE IS MINE

If we give up and turn our backs on all we've learned, all we've been given, all the truth we now know, we repudiate Christ's sacrifice and are left on our own to face the Judgment—and a mighty fierce judgment it will be! If the penalty for breaking the law of Moses is physical death, what do you think will happen if you turn on God's Son, spit on the sacrifice that made you whole, and insult this most gracious Spirit? This is no light matter. God has warned us that he'll hold us to account and make us pay. He was quite explicit: "Vengeance is mine, and I won't overlook a thing" and "God will judge his people." Nobody's getting by with anything, believe me (Hebrews 10:26-31 The Message).

THIS Scripture passage is certainly quite clear about what God's judgment will be if we turn our back on the Gospel. I can't imagine that any of us want to be "left on our own to face the Judgment" that He would mete out to those who "spit on the sacrifice" and "insult this most gracious Spirit." We must be cautious not to abuse this Spirit of Grace when we speak and act. Always giving praise and showing adoration to God assures us that His vengeance will not be aimed at us.

Take Away for Today

1. Is it reassuring or frightening to know that God doesn't "overlook a thing" and that "Nobody's getting by with anything"?
2. Is it ever right for you to mete out revenge against a person for a wrong?

DO NOT INSULT
THE SPIRIT OF GRACE

*How much more severely do you think a man deserves to
be punished who has trampled the Son of God under foot,
who has treated as an unholy thing the blood of the covenant
that sanctified him, and who has insulted the Spirit of grace?*
(Hebrews 10:29)

THE blood Christ shed on the cross is our atonement. Our
redemption is based on His sacrifice on the cross and our
acknowledgment of it. We deserve punishment if we toss aside as
unimportant the Son of God, His blood, and the grace of God that
put Him on the cross. Be careful not to take for granted the magnitude of this sacrifice.

Take Away for Today

1. Have you ever insulted the Spirit of Grace? What were
    the consequences?

2. Did you repent and seek forgiveness?

THE "LET US" CONSIDERATION

Therefore, brothers and sisters...let us draw near to God with a sincere heart and with the full assurance that faith brings.... Let us hold unswervingly to the hope we profess, for he who promised is faithful. And let us consider how we may spur one another on toward love and good deeds, not giving up meeting together, as some are in the habit of doing, but encouraging one another—and all the more as you see the Day approaching (Hebrews 10:19-25).

LET us draw near to God; let us hold to the hope; let us cheer each other on toward love and good deeds. This passage is full of "Let us"—good advice from the writer of Hebrews. Let us take seriously these Scripture verses from His Word and then do what it says including meeting together and encouraging each other.

Take Away for Today

1. Can you think of additional "Let us" examples that fall in line with this Kingdom mindset?

2. Have you made it a habit to meet together with other believers? Or have you given up meeting together?

Reading the Bible in a Year: Proverbs 19-20 and 2 Corinthians 3.

DON'T THROW AWAY
YOUR CONFIDENCE

*So **do not throw away your confidence; it will be richly
rewarded**. You need to persevere so that when you have done
the will of God, **you will receive what he has promised.** For
in just a very little while, **he who is coming will come** and
will not delay* (Hebrews 10:35-37).

I F the Hebrews had to be told not to throw away their confidence,
it stands to reason that there were some who must have done
just that. They must have been discouraged or passive, lacking self-
esteem. This is not an uncommon life situation, so whatever may
want to steal your confidence, don't throw it away!

Take Away for Today

1. Are you easily discouraged? Are you tired of persevering?

2. What is it you are looking forward to receiving?

3. Does knowing that Jesus will return at the appointed
   time bring hope...or just a wondering?

_____

_____

_____

THE RIGHTEOUS LIVE BY FAITH

Remember those early days after you first saw the light? Those were the hard times! Kicked around in public, targets of every kind of abuse—some days it was you, other days your friends. If some friends went to prison, you stuck by them. If some enemies broke in and seized your goods, you let them go with a smile, knowing they couldn't touch your real treasure. Nothing they did bothered you, nothing set you back. So don't throw it all away now. You were sure of yourselves then. It's still a sure thing! But you need to stick it out, staying with God's plan so you'll be there for the promised completion. It won't be long now, he's on the way; he'll show up most any minute. But anyone who is right with me thrives on loyal trust; if he cuts and runs, I won't be very happy. But we're not quitters who lose out. Oh, no! We'll stay with it and survive, trusting all the way (Hebrews 10:32-39 The Message).

THIS familiar Scripture passage gets an extra boost of meaning from The Message version. I encourage you to read it several times. The righteous, the just, live by faith. We must be as sure of our faith and our commitment to Him now as we were back when we were new believers. Living by faith means living on trust.

Take Away for Today

1. Are you living on faith?
2. Are you trusting God with all your heart, mind, and soul?

DO NOT LOSE HEART

Therefore we do not lose heart. Though outwardly we are wasting away, yet inwardly we are being renewed day by day (2 Corinthians 4:16).

THE older people get, the more their bodies show the wear and tear of existing in this world of deterioration. But! Our inner beings can be renewed and refreshed every day, bringing newness and fresh life within us. This is a glorious realization as we look in the mirror and don't recognize that face which may have a few more wrinkles each day. Rejoice in your beautiful or handsome spiritual self—and do not lose heart!

Take Away for Today

1. Do you sometimes lose heart because you see yourself wasting away?

2. Can you take comfort in the fact that your inner self— the important eternal self—is being renewed every day when you praise God, read and obey His Word, and seek His presence?

DIVINE HOME SECURITY

*You need not worry about your home while you are gone; nothing
shall be stolen from your barns* (Job 5:24 The Living Bible).

THE world is fast becoming a global village and inevitably many
are separated from their homes and their loved ones. Sometimes
a job takes someone away from loved ones, other times loved ones
may go away in pursuit of education and training. This Scripture
from Job is refreshing for these moments of unavoidable separation.
This is a divine promise that whatever the reason for you being away
from home, when you return you shall find nothing missing!

David said in Psalm 37:25, *"I was young and now I am old, yet I
have never seen righteous forsaken or their children begging bread."*
Your descendants shall not beg for bread and are secured even when
you are away from them!

Take Away for Today

1. Are you fearful whenever you have to leave your home
   for an extended time? Why?
2. Does this verse bring you comfort? Will you leave your
   home the next time feeling more secure?

NO MORE GROPING
OR STUMBLING

You groped your way through that murk once, but no longer. You're out in the open now. The bright light of Christ makes your way plain. So no more stumbling around. Get on with it! The good, the right, the true—these are the actions appropriate for daylight hours. Figure out what will please Christ, and then do it (Ephesians 5:8-10 The Message).

GOD is the Father of Light, and we are the children of Light. And because of the fruits of the Light, we are empowered not groping or stumbling anymore. God is the bright Light that shines before us as we walk through life holding His hand all the way. There should be no more stumbling around for us because we are always in His light of goodness, righteousness, and truth. Walk confidently and proudly today, out in the open, as a child of the Light.

Take Away for Today

1. Do you hold your head up so His light can shine on your face as you walk together toward your destiny?

2. Are you tired of groping and stumbling around in the dark? Are you ready to take action!

THE BLABBER OF THE WICKED

Liars secretly hoard hatred; fools openly spread slander. The more talk, the less truth; the wise measure their words. The speech of a good person is worth waiting for; the blabber of the wicked is worthless (Proverbs 10:18-20).

I T is hard to believe and harder to admit, but there are people who lie without giving it a second thought. There are those who have no conscience when it comes to lying or "stretching the truth" as some describe it.

Take Away for Today

1. Are you suspicious of people who talk too much?
2. Is your speech worth waiting for?

BECAUSE OF FAITH

Because of faith Enoch was caught up and transferred to heaven, so that he did not have a glimpse of death; and he was not found, because God had translated him. For even before he was taken to heaven, he received testimony [still on record] that he had pleased and been satisfactory to God
(Hebrews 11:5 AMP).

BECAUSE of faith Enoch was taken to heaven without even dying! Because God found Enoch pleasing and satisfactory, he didn't have to experience any pain or suffering as some do prior to leaving this world for the next. Faith is the key to finding favor with God.

Take Away for Today

1. How strong is your faith today? As strong as Enoch's faith?

2. If God did this for Enoch who was merely "satisfactory" to God, what do you think God can do for those who are "extraordinary" to Him?

FAITH AND THE UNSEEN WORLD

By faith—by believing God—we know that the world and the stars—in fact, all things—were made at God's command; and that they were all made from things that can't be seen (Hebrews 11:3 The Living Bible).

FAITH'S role in the spiritual realm is more vital than anything seen or heard in the natural world. To have faith when believing that God created the world and the heavens is to know beyond the shadow of a doubt that the truth lies within the pages of the Bible and in the sound of His voice. There is an unseen world—a spiritual realm that exists. And faith is the currency by which you can purchase things in the unseen world!

Take Away for Today

1. By faith do you believe that God created all things seen from what can't be seen?

2. By faith do you believe that all will be revealed in the twinkling of His eye?

_____

_____

_____

OBEDIENCE TO THE FAITH

*And the message of God kept on spreading, and the number
of disciples multiplied greatly in Jerusalem; and [besides] a
large number of the priests were obedient to the faith [in Jesus
as the Messiah, through Whom is obtained eternal salvation
in the kingdom of God]* (Acts 6:7 AMP).

E VEN those who are zealous about another faith or are convinced
that there is no God can be turned around toward the light and
life of Jesus when the gospel is shared at the right time and with the
leading of the Holy Spirit. In this verse in Acts, it says the number of
followers of the Lord Jesus Christ increased greatly and even priests
came to know Him as their Savior—they became obedient to the
faith. Hallelujah!

Take Away for Today

1. What does being obedient to the faith mean to you?
   Write a definition.
2. Have you witnessed a conversion that was an amazing example of a person turning from falsehood to the
   Truth?

_____

_____

_____

KEEP YOUR EYES ON JESUS

Keep your eyes on Jesus, our leader and instructor. He was willing to die a shameful death on the cross because of the joy he knew would be his afterwards; and now he sits in the place of honor by the throne of God. If you want to keep from becoming fainthearted and weary, think about his patience as sinful men did such terrible things to him (Hebrews 12:2-3 The Living Bible).

HERE the Bible again refers to believers possibly becoming weary and fainthearted. The Bible says in due season we shall reap if we don't faint (see Gal. 6:9). I suggest we take this advice seriously and determine not to become tired of believing and living the Kingdom life. After all, the alternative is bondage and possibly eternal damnation.

Take Away for Today

1. When you are keeping your eyes on Jesus, are you concentrating on Him or is your mind wondering and wandering?

2. If you are going through challenges and troubles, can you look beyond to afterward when you will sit in the place of honor with your brother, Jesus?

FOCUS ON THE THINGS ABOVE

Since, then, you have been raised with Christ, set your hearts on things above, where Christ is, seated at the right hand of God. Set your minds on things above, not on earthly things. For you died, and your life is now hidden with Christ in God (Colossians 3:1-3).

WHILE we are keeping our eyes on Jesus, let us also set our minds on things above—not worldly, earthly things. The more we think about good godly things and do good godly acts, the more we will be prepared to sit with Jesus at the right hand of God.

Take Away for Today

1. What are some of the things above on which you can focus? Name several.

2. What are some earthly, worldly things on which you should not focus?

3. Now erase or strike through the list you wrote for #1 and delete them from your mind, replacing them with the list from #2.

FOCUS ON THE ETERNAL

So we do not look at what we can see right now, the troubles all around us, but we look forward to the joys in heaven which we have not yet seen. The troubles will soon be over, but the joys to come will last forever (2 Corinthians 4:18 The Living Bible).

WHEN we focus on our troubles and toils, they loom much larger and more menacing than need be. When we look forward to the joys in heaven that await us, our mindset is lightened and burdens relieved. Remember, today's troubles will soon be over—but our joy in Christ will last forever!

Take Away for Today

1. What is the best way to lighten your load?
2. What is the second best way to lighten your load?

_____

_____

_____

RELAX—DON'T WORRY

If God gives such attention to the appearance of wildflowers—most of which are never even seen—don't you think he'll attend to you, take pride in you, do his best for you? What I'm trying to do here is to get you to relax, to not be so preoccupied with getting, so you can respond to God's giving. People who don't know God and the way he works fuss over these things, but you know both God and how he works. Steep your life in God-reality, God-initiative, God-provisions. Don't worry about missing out. You'll find all your everyday human concerns will be met (Matthew 6:30-33 The Message).

THIS version of the "Seek first His Kingdom and His righteousness, and all these things will be given to you" passage in Matthew expands the traditional verses, going deeper into the actual aspects of the thought. How does this expanded version settle within your heart and mind? It is good for us not to so preoccupied with getting that we cannot relax and enjoy the giving.

Take Away for Today

1. How good are you at seeking His kingdom and His righteousness?

2. How good are you at wanting to receive all the good and righteous things He has for you?

How Well God Must Like You

How well God must like you—you don't hang out at Sin Saloon, you don't slink along Dead-End Road, you don't go to Smart-Mouth College. Instead you thrill to God's Word, you chew on Scripture day and night. You're a tree replanted in Eden, bearing fresh fruit every month, never dropping a leaf, always in blossom (Psalm 1:1-3 The Message).

ALTHOUGH some of the language in these verses seems to be humorous, it is addressing serious spiritual business. Perhaps you are more familiar with the New King James Version of this passage, "Blessed is the man who walks not in the counsel of the ungodly, nor stands in the path of sinners, nor sits in the seat of the scornful; but his delight is in the law of the Lord, and in His law he meditates day and night. He shall be like a tree planted by the rivers of water that brings forth its fruit in its season, whose leaf also shall not wither; and whatever he does shall prosper." Either version, the message is clear: God wants us to read and meditate on the Bible, stay away from sin, and enjoy prosperity.

Take Away for Today

1. Do you visit the Sin Saloon on a regular basis?
2. Are you habitually walking down Dead-End Road?
3. Did you graduate from Smart-Mouth College?

Reading the Bible in a Year: Isaiah 4-6 and Galatians 3.

A Time of Thanksgiving

These things I remember as I pour out my soul: how I used to go to the house of God under the protection of the Mighty One with shouts of joy and praise among the festive throng (Psalm 42:4).

"SHOUTS of joy and praise among the festive throng" brings to mind a wonderful celebration. Everyone likes to be part of such an occasion. People are attracted to festivities that include singing and dancing and joyfulness. Christians need to generate times like these to reveal God's true nature. We need not sit around with gloom and doom faces—let us rejoice in the Lord!

Take Away for Today

1. Are you ready to put on a smile and wear it every day, sharing it with all you meet?

2. Can you generate a festive environment within your home, your church, your workplace that proves your God is a God of joy and good times?

GOD KNOWS US INSIDE AND OUT

But Jesus would not entrust himself to them,
for he knew all people (John 2:24).

THE Message version of the Bible interprets this verse this way: "During the time he was in Jerusalem, those days of the Passover Feast, many people noticed the signs he was displaying and, seeing they pointed straight to God, entrusted their lives to him. But Jesus didn't entrust his life to them. He knew them inside and out, knew how untrustworthy they were. He didn't need any help in seeing right through them." Isn't it interesting that John realized Jesus' insights into the people at the feast? Of course Jesus knew them inside and out—just like He knows us that intimately.

Take Away for Today

1. What does Jesus see when He looks at you inside and out?

2. Do you think He would entrust His life to you?

September 28

YOUR LIFE
BACK TOGETHER

*Why is everyone hungry for more? "More, more," they say.
"More, more." I have God's more-than-enough, more joy in
one ordinary day than they get in all their shopping sprees.
At day's end I'm ready for sound sleep, for you, God, have put
my life back together* (Psalm 4:6-8 The Message).

I T is human nature to want more, more. More money, more clothing, more cars, more vacations—more, more, more! We have insatiable appetites for more, thinking that more of this or that will bring us happiness, will fill the void that only the Holy Spirit within us can fill. God is more than enough! Today, and every day, rest in God and let Him put your life back together.

Take Away for Today

1.   Are you hungry for more?
2.   Will having more worldly things and stuff bring you the joy that one moment in His presence can bring?

_____

_____

_____

September 29

Not all are God's Children

You belong to your father, the devil, and you want to carry out
your father's desires. He was a murderer from the beginning,
not holding to the truth, for there is no truth in him. When
he lies, he speaks his native language, for he is a liar and the
father of lies (John 8:44).

ALTHOUGH we don't want to admit it, unless we are totally committed and fully given over to the Lord, then we are children of the devil. There are only two options: we belong to the family of God or the torments of the devil. Let us choose today to be with the One who loves us and wishes us only goodness and grace.

Take Away for Today

1. There is no truth in the evil one's words. Do you sometimes get pulled into his lies?
2. Can you tell God's truth from the devil's lies?

THE HOUR WHEN DARKNESS REIGNS

[Jesus said] *"Every day I was with you in the temple courts, and you did not lay a hand on me. But this is your hour— when darkness reigns"* (Luke 22:53).

THE hour when darkness reigns is the horror of our imaginations. For Jesus, the time came for Him to be arrested, then denied by Peter, then tortured and murdered. When darkness reigns, people are afraid and don't know which way to turn. Their minds become confused—and the devil preys on them. But! Jesus didn't stay in the grave, He overcame death, and He walked among the people once again. Forever He destroyed darkness—never again should it occupy our minds. Turn to Him if you experience the hour when darkness reigns, and live in the light!

Take Away for Today

1. Does darkness reign in your life from time to time? What causes this?

2. Determine today to rid every bit of darkness from your body, mind, and soul by shining God's light throughout your life.

RESCUE ME!

I come to you for protection, O Lord my God. Save me from my persecutors—rescue me! If you don't, they will maul me like a lion, tearing me to pieces with no one to rescue me. O Lord my God, if I have done wrong or am guilty of injustice, if I have betrayed a friend or plundered my enemy without cause, then let my enemies capture me. Let them trample me into the ground and drag my honor in the dust (Psalm 7:1-5 NLT).

ALTHOUGH David, the psalmist, was pleading for protection from God, he was still cognizant of his role in the circumstances. When we ask for protection, are we as humble as David to acknowledge our actions that may have caused our problems? It is wise to use this passage as a guide when we are asking God to rescue us from our persecutors.

Take Away for Today

1. When being persecuted by others, do you take the time to search yourself for possible causes?

2. Do you ask God to search you and expose any wrongdoings that may be causing you to become the target of persecution?

MISPLACED PRIORITY

For they loved human praise more than praise from God
(John 12:43).

M ANY times it is easy for we humans to want to bask in the accolades of our co-workers, a boss, our family, and even people we don't even know. We enjoy when our deeds are noticed and brought to the attention of others. Pride is a subtle and very useful tool of the evil one. We so quickly succumb to our selfish side. But how long does our puffed up feelings last? A week? A day? A moment? Then what is left? Emptiness until the next pride-high. Pride is like a fist in the face of God! When we seek praise from God, there is a lasting feeling of love and joy—a genuine exchange of respect.

Take Away for Today

1. Are you guilty of seeking approval and praise from others rather than God?

2. Do you acknowledge others' accomplishments with a godly attitude?

_____

_____

_____

ANDREW THE FACILITATOR

The next day John was there again with two of his disciples.
When he saw Jesus passing by, he said, "Look, the Lamb of
God!" ...Andrew, Simon Peter's brother, was one of the two
who heard what John had said and who had followed Jesus.
The first thing Andrew did was to find his brother Simon and
tell him, "We have found the Messiah" (that is, the Christ).
And he brought him to Jesus... (John 1:35-42).

A NDREW was eager to share the Lord with others. He thought
it was so important that the "first thing" he did "was to find his
brother and tell him." When we know the Lord Jesus Christ, we too
must think it is very important—important enough to share the good
news with everyone we know. "And he brought him to Jesus," just as
we need to do. Facilitate someone toward Jesus Christ today.

Take Away for Today

1. Are you a facilitator like Andrew? Do you make things
   happen in and for the Kingdom?
2. When was the last time you showed someone the way
   to Jesus?

ANDREW—THE IMPLEMENTER

Another of his disciples, Andrew, Simon Peter's brother, spoke up, "Here is a boy with five small barley loaves and two small fish, but how far will they go among so many?" (John 6:8-9)

ANDREW was with Jesus when the crowd of more than 5,000 was listening to Him teach. When Jesus realized that the people needed nourishment, Andrew was the one who found the young boy who had only a few loaves of bread and two little fish. Andrew didn't look the other way when he saw the small amount of food the boy had, rather he brought the boy to Jesus—hoping for a miracle. Be an implementer of God's purpose today.

Take Away for Today

1.   Do you see the possibility in impossible situations?
2.   Can you look beyond what is right before you in the natural into the unknown spiritual realm of possibilities?

ON THE SIDE OF TRUTH

*"You are a king, then!" said Pilate. Jesus answered, "You are right that I am a king. In fact, the reason I was born and came into the world is to **testify to the truth. Everyone on the side of truth listens to me**" (John 18:37).*

"EVERYONE on the side of truth listens to me," Jesus said. These days many claim to have "the truth." From selling products in stores and on television to leaders of the many various faiths worldwide. But only God's Word has stood the test of time and touches hearts so deeply that Jesus is the name still held above all other names—centuries after His death and resurrection. He is the Truth, the Way, and the Life! For I have decided I will be on the side of the truth.

Take Away for Today

1. Are you swayed by someone claiming to have the "real truth"?
2. How many "truths" can there be?

_____

_____

_____

GREATER IS GOD IN YOU

Little children, you are of God [you belong to Him] and have [already] defeated and overcome them [the agents of the antichrist], because He Who lives in you is greater (mightier) than he who is in the world (1 John 4:4 AMP).

THIS verse has been a comfort to many over many years. To know that God in us is greater than the evil in the world gives us hope and peace that we will make it through the next challenge that we face, that we will overcome the trial we are going through, that we are moving closer to God in all His glory every time we acknowledge His presence. We are of God and have already defeated the enemy!

Take Away for Today

1. Have you memorized First John 4:4? I encourage you do to so.

2. Has this verse been especially helpful for you to remember during times of trials? Do you believe it's truth with all of your heart and mind?

October 7

A SENSE OF DESTINY

Then Paul answered, "Why are you weeping and breaking my heart? I am ready not only to be bound, but also to die in Jerusalem for the name of the Lord Jesus" (Acts 21:13).

PAUL—THE one who persecuted Christians then was converted, the one who wrote many of the books in the New Testament—was ready to die for the name of the Lord Jesus. He wasn't afraid of dying for what he believed to be the truth—that Jesus was the Son of God and He died and rose to redeem all of humankind. Paul endured much to spread the good news. He had a sense of destiny that drove him on toward his great reward of knowing others accepted the Truth and that he would spend eternity with his Lord and Savior.

Take Away for Today

1. Does your sense of destiny drive you toward your great reward?

2. Are you willing to die for your faith in God, and Jesus the Son of God?

A LIFE DEVOTED

However, I consider my life worth nothing to me, my only aim is to finish the race and complete the task the Lord Jesus has given me—the task of testifying to the good news of God's grace (Acts 20:24).

PAUL considered his life "worth nothing" except that he would use it to finish his task to share the good news of Jesus with others. He was determined to tell everyone possible what he knew about the Lord. His aim was focused and his mission clearly defined. He had devoted his life to revealing the message of salvation to as many people as possible—knowing their eternal souls were at stake. Paul's devotion to God is worthy of emulation.

Take Away for Today

1. When people meet you, do they sense a life devoted to Christ?
2. Do you consider your life worth nothing except to share the good news?

THE GENTLEMAN CALLED CORNELIUS

There was a certain man in Caesarea called Cornelius, a centurion of what was called the Italian Regiment, a devout man and one who feared God with all his household, who gave alms generously to the people, and prayed to God always (Acts 10:1 NKJV).

CORNELIUS was a good man; he loved God and helped people in need. He had a visitation from an angel saying that, "Your prayers and your alms have come up for a memorial before God." The angel also told him other things which led to Peter's vision about what to eat. The entire story, starting with the good, gentle man Cornelius, ends with a new revelation and the Holy Spirit falling on the Gentiles. Praise God for good people who watch and listen for angels sent from God and obey what God commands!

Take Away for Today

1. Are you one who watches, listens, and obeys?
2. Do you realize that at any moment you may be the one God chooses to use in an extraordinary way?

DON'T BE AFRAID

*One night the Lord spoke to Paul in a vision: "Do not be afraid; **keep on speaking, do not be silent. For I am with you,** and no one is going to attack and harm you, because I have many people in this city"* (Acts 18:9-10).

PAUL was sound asleep one night when the Lord chose to speak to him through a vision. What Paul heard was no doubt a welcome voice and a very welcome message saying that he would be safe—that the Lord would protect him if he kept speaking, kept sharing the good news of Christ alive. "For I am with you," were probably the sweetest words he could have heard at that time.

Take Away for Today

1. Are you afraid of what people will say if your share your faith with them?

2. God tells us not to be afraid and that He is with us; are you listening?

_____

_____

_____

BRING IT ON!

The night is nearly over; the day is almost here. So let us put aside the deeds of darkness and put on the armor of light (Romans 13:12).

WE have discussed God's light that shines on our path through life, we have also discussed that we are the light of the world. Now in this verse Paul is contending that we can actually "put on the armor of light"! Light as a protective covering means that it will deflect the jabs and arrows of the enemy. Light is capable of completely encompassing every inch of us from the top of our heads to the tips of our toes—one size fits all. Bring it on!

Take Away for Today

1. Are you ready to don your suit of light and face any new challenge of the day?
2. Can you see the advantages of wearing a full-length armor of light to deflect anything the enemy throws at you?

IRREVOCABLE GIFTS AND CALLING

for God's gifts and his call are irrevocable (Romans 11:29).

"GOD'S *gifts and God's call are under full warranty—never canceled, never rescinded*" (Romans 11:29 The Message). God loves us so much that when He makes a promise and places a calling on your life, you are guaranteed their actualization. Every gift has a name tag on it; every promise will be fulfilled; every calling will make the Kingdom of God richer. All we have to do is follow His voice.

Take Away for Today

1. How firm are the promises or gifts that the world offers?
2. Are you excited about receiving all the gifts and promises He wants to give you?

LOVE NEVER FAILS

*Let no debt remain outstanding, except the continuing debt
to **love one another,** for whoever loves others has
fulfilled the law* (Romans 13:8).

ALTHOUGH our heavenly Father has so lavishly promised us gifts including an abundant life, the only debt we owe Him in return is the "continuing debt to love one another." Only God would consider this appropriate compensation for all that He has done for us. Only Jesus would require such a payment for all that He went through to provide eternal life for us.

Take Away for Today

1. Are you willing to daily pay your debt of loving others?
2. When you find it hard to love someone, can you take time to remember this verse and change your mind?

CONSCIENCE-STRICKEN

Afterward, David was conscience-stricken for having cut off a corner of his [Saul's] *robe (1 Samuel 24:5).*

DAVID'S conscience bothered him for cutting a piece of Saul's robe. Why did this bother David? *"Now it happened afterward that David's heart troubled him because he had cut Saul's robe. And he said to his men, 'The Lord forbid that I should do this thing to my master, the Lord's anointed, to stretch out my hand against him, seeing he is the anointed of the Lord'"* (1 Sam. 24:5-6 NKJV). We must be cautious when taking any action against another believer or leader. God knows the beginning from the end and we must not stymie His plan.

Take Away for Today

1. Have you ever been "conscience-stricken"?
2. Have you had bouts of a guilty conscience because of something you said or did when you realized it went against righteousness?

_____

_____

_____

GOD DID NOT GIVE HIM UP

David stayed in the wilderness strongholds and in the hills of the Desert of Ziph. Day after day Saul searched for him, but God did not give David into his hands (1 Samuel 23:14).

KING Saul was searching for David to kill him. But God did not allow Saul to find David, for David was an important part of God's plan of redemption of humankind. We also play important roles in God's plan to gather as many souls into eternity as possible. He will not allow the enemy to thwart our destiny, and He will not give us into the enemy's hands.

Take Away for Today

1. Has the enemy been stalking you day after day?
2. Have you been seeking shelter in the wilderness strongholds and hills that the Lord provided for your safety?

THE ROCK OF ESCAPE

Then Saul went on one side of the mountain, and David and his men on the other side of the mountain. So David made haste to get away from Saul, for Saul and his men were encircling David and his men to take them. But a messenger came to Saul, saying, "Hurry and come, for the Philistines have invaded the land!" Therefore Saul returned from pursuing David, and went against the Philistines; so they called that place the Rock of Escape. Then David went up from there and dwelt in strongholds at En Gedi (1 Samuel 23:26-29 NKJV).

GOD once again saved David from danger and death. Saul was determined to rid himself of David, but when he heard that the Philistines were invading his land, Saul forgot about David. The Rock of Escape was named as such because David realized that God used this place as a safe refuge—an escape from great danger! Whatever may be challenging you at this moment, God will raise a rock of escape for you!

Take Away for Today

1. Do you have a rock of escape? A place where God saved you from destruction?

2. Where is your safe refuge?

3. Has God revealed a place where you can feel safe and secure?

_____

_____

GOD ANSWERED
ABIGAIL'S PRAYERS

Please forgive your servant's presumption. The Lord your God will certainly make a lasting dynasty for my lord...but the lives of your enemies he will hurl away as from the pocket of a sling. Then David accepted from her hand what she had brought him and said, "Go home in peace. I have heard your words and granted your request" (1 Samuel 25:28-29,35).

ABIGAIL was bold enough to approach David and his band of men. She knew that they were capable of avenging and bloodshed. David heard her word and granted her request. Her confidence should be motivation and encouragement for us when we are facing woes and foes. Abigail had many answered prayers. God indeed established a lasting dynasty for David. Also David's enemy (Nabal) had his life hurled "away as from the pocket of a sling"; *"About ten days later, the Lord struck Nabal and he died"* (1 Samuel 25:38).

May God always hear and answer your prayers!

Take Away for Today

1. Can you muster enough boldness to say what needs to be said?

2. Can you "go home in peace" after speaking your mind, with respect and sincerity?

SLEEP SENT FROM GOD

So David took the spear and water jug near Saul's head, and they left. No one saw or knew about it, nor did anyone wake up. They were all sleeping, because the Lord had put them into a deep sleep (1 Samuel 26:12).

THE Lord put Saul and his army into a deep sleep so David could sneak down into the camp. When David and Abishai approached Saul, it was obvious that he could easily be killed, thus ending the seemingly never-ending searching and hiding. But David stopped Abishai from harming Saul, saying, *"Don't destroy him! Who can lay a hand on the LORD's anointed and be guiltless? As surely as the LORD lives,"* he said, *"the LORD himself will strike him, or his time will come and he will die, or he will go into battle and perish. But the LORD forbid that I should lay a hand on the LORD's anointed."* David was more focused on the Lord than he was on his own safety. The question that must be asked is why did God send the deep sleep? On the surface it may seem to deliver Saul and his army into David's hand, but beneath the surface it was actually to test David. Had he killed Saul because it was within his power, he could have still become the king even sooner—but then he would never have become the man after God's heart!

Take Away for Today

1. Are you more focused on the Lord than your own safety or problems?
2. Even though you may be in harm's way, are you sleeping peacefully knowing that the Lord is on your side?

GOD BESTOWS HIS POWER

And David became more and more powerful, because the Lord God of Heaven's Armies was with him (2 Samuel 5:10 NLT).

"HEAVEN'S Armies" has a nice ring to it! Oh that we are soldiers enough to be included in such a prestigious group. David had been running and hiding and battling for a very long time; and then God, in His infinite mercy, bestowed His power upon David. God, as the Commander of Heaven's Armies, proved once again that only He can claim victory over evil.

Take Away for Today

1. Do you feel powerful? If not, why?
2. What do you need to feel powerful?
3. How can you gain spiritual power?

SELF-EVIDENT

Then David knew that the Lord had established him as king over Israel and had exalted his kingdom for the sake of his people Israel (2 Samuel 5:12).

WHEN we know that we know God has spoken to us, then we need to stand firm on that word. It will be self-evident what God wants us to do, say, or be. We must be willing to "know" what it is He desires of us and then take action to show our obedience. If we listen carefully for His voice and our heart's confirmation, it will be spiritually self-evident that we are going in the right direction.

Take Away for Today

1. Have you had a self-evident event such as David's?
2. Has the Lord established you in a certain situation? Family? Career?

_____

_____

_____

DISCERNING THE VOICES OF GOD

But Jehoshaphat asked, "Is there not also a prophet of the Lord here? We should ask him the same question" (1 Kings 22:7 NLT).

THIS is one of the securities we enjoy as born-again believers, that the Spirit of God in us will prompt us to the presence of falsehood or when we encounter demonic utterances. Something was unsettled inside Jehoshaphat when he heard the false prophecies. Jehoshaphat wanted to make certain that what was heard was actually from the Lord. Although about 400 prophets told Jehoshaphat and King Ahab that they would have victory, Jehoshaphat wanted one more opinion. Micaiah was called and contradicted the other prophets' prediction. It is always best to seek the Lord directly when facing an important decision.

Take Away for Today

1. How can you tell when it is the Lord speaking to you?
2. What tests can you use to determine, discern, the Lord's voice from others?

THE TURN OF EVENTS WAS FROM THE LORD

*So the king paid no attention to the people. **This turn of events was the will of the Lord, for it fulfilled the Lord's message** to Jeroboam son of Nebat through the prophet Ahijah from Shiloh* (1 Kings 12:15 NLT).

J UST when we think we have something all planned out and are ready to proceed, sometimes the Lord has a better plan and there is a turn of events. We have to be flexible when the Lord steps in with a better way, a better day. The problem is that sometimes such turn of events may not appear as if from God! Being too rigid in our thinking may mean we miss out on something very special that the Lord had in mind for us.

Take Away for Today

1. How flexible are you when it comes to changing your plans?
2. Can you accept change graciously or do you tend to resist change?

GOD'S WRATH IS DIRECTED AT THE DEVIL

The king of Israel said to Jehoshaphat, "As we go into battle, I will disguise myself so no one will recognize me, but you wear your royal robes." So the king of Israel disguised himself, and they went into battle (1 Kings 22:30 NLT).

ALTHOUGH the king of Israel, Ahab, was going into battle together with the king of Judah, Jehoshaphat, against Ramoth-gilead, Ahab plotted and wanted Jehoshaphat to be the enemy's target, asking him to wear the royal robes. As it turned out, an enemy soldier randomly shot an arrow into the Israelite group of troops that mortally wounded King Ahab. It is no use to think we can hide from God's watchful eyes. The intrigue of humans can prevail as the wisdom of God.

Take Away for Today

1. What was Ahab's ultimate goal?
2. Do you know people who always have their own agenda at the forefront?
3. How do these people usually end up?

DAVID'S CLOSE WALK WITH GOD

*After this, David asked the Lord, "Should I move back to one
of the towns of Judah?" "Yes," the Lord replied. Then David
asked, "Which town should I go to?" "To Hebron," the Lord
answered* (2 Samuel 2:1).

D AVID was close to the Lord because his attention was focused
almost always on his heavenly Father. In this verse, David didn't
just ask God if he should move, but also asked to which town he
should move. As long as our focus is on God, we do good things and
God is for us. But the moment we take our eyes off God and onto
fleshly desires, God removes His protection. Even for David, a man
after God's own heart (see 2 Sam. 11:26—12:19).

Take Away for Today

1. How closely are you walking with God?
2. Have you shielded your eyes and heart from whatever
   is not of God?

AN EVIL ALLIANCE
WILL NOT WORK

*Some time later King Jehoshaphat of Judah made an alliance with King Ahaziah of Israel, who was very wicked. Together they built a fleet of trading ships at the port of Ezion-geber. Then Eliezer son of Dodavahu from Mareshah prophesied against Jehoshaphat. He said, "**Because you have allied yourself with King Ahaziah, the Lord will destroy your work**." So the ships met with disaster and never put out to sea* (2 Chronicles 20:35-37 NLT).

KING Jehoshaphat again allied himself with a scoundrel. And this time the Lord destroyed his work—his fleet of trading ships. We must not allow ourselves to be taken in by flattery and the talk of "good deals" if we know in our hearts that the partnership is not one made in heaven. Who and what we align ourselves with matters very much to God—and should matter very much to us. Beware!

Take Away for Today

1. Have you joined forces with someone who let you down?
2. Was the disappointment surprising, or did you know deep down that it would not work out in the long term?

_____

_____

_____

ELISHA'S RASHNESS AND INTOLERANCE

...Elisha turned around and looked at them, and he cursed them in the name of the Lord. Then two bears came out of the woods and mauled forty-two of them. ...When Gehazi left the room, he was covered with leprosy; his skin was white as snow. ...And so it was, for the people trampled him to death at the gate! (2 Kings 2:23-24; 5:26-27; 7:18-20 NLT)

ELISHA had the double portion of the anointing of Elijah and performed twice as many miracles as Elijah did. Despite the anointing in his life, he was unable to overcome intolerance and rash utterances. He called bears to maul forty-two youths, he left his servant, Gehazi, leprous, the man on whose shoulder the king's rest was trampled to death, and on Elisha's death bed he was angry with King Jehoash of Israel and limited the king's victories to only three! (See 2 Kings 13:15-19.) All these things happened by the power of the anointing of Elisha's words. Anointing needs to be carried by a crucified and mature character. Spend time to prepare yourself for what God prepared for you!

Take Away for Today

1. Why is it that some people who are anointed fail to continue walking in God's ways?
2. What is your theory about why Elisha ended his life so miserably when he started out with a double portion of Elijah's anointing?

_____

_____

THE LORD GIVES REST

When King David was settled in his palace and the Lord had given him rest from all the surrounding enemies, the king summoned Nathan the prophet. "Look," David said, "I am living in a beautiful cedar palace, but the Ark of God is out there in a tent!" Nathan replied to the king, "Go ahead and do whatever you have in mind, for the Lord is with you" (2 Samuel 7:1-3 NLT).

Finally David was settled in the palace and the Lord gave him rest. But rather than relaxing and forgetting about the Lord, David called for Nathan and spoke to him about the Ark of God. David was concerned about the opulence in which he was living while the presence of God remained in a common tent. As we rest in our modern-day opulence, let us remember that God desires to be with us.

Take Away for Today

1. Do you welcome God's presence into your home, your bedroom, your workplace?

2. Are you joyful knowing that God's Ark is now residing within you?

WASH AND BE CLEAN

But Naaman became angry and stalked away. "I thought he
would certainly come out to meet me!" he said. "I expected him
to wave his hand over the leprosy and call on the name of the
Lord his God and heal me! Aren't the rivers of Damascus, the
Abana and the Pharpar, better than any of the rivers of Israel?
Why shouldn't I wash in them and be healed?" So Naaman
turned and went away in a rage (2 Kings 5:11-12 NLT).

NAAMAN was suffering from leprosy and wanted to be healed. But Naaman's pride got in the way when Elisha, the prophet who was willing and able to heal him, did not come out to meet him. Naaman thought that dipping himself in the Jordan River was not the way to healing, but after his maid convinced him, Naaman went and did as he was told—and he was healed. May wrong mindsets and prejudice not limit your breakthroughs in God!

Take Away for Today

1. Do you allow your pride to get in the way of being healed?

2. Has God or one of His messengers brought you instructions that made you balk?

THE GREATEST OF ALL COMFORT

This, at least, gives me comfort despite all the pain—that I have not denied the words of the holy God (Job 6:10 The Living Bible).

LIKE Job's wife there are life situations that threaten to compel us to deny God. Job's wife asked him to "curse God and die". This was Job's testimony: *"His wife said to him, 'Are you still maintaining your integrity? Curse God and die!' He replied, 'You are talking like a foolish woman. Shall we accept good from God, and not trouble?' In all this, Job did not sin in what he said"* (Job 2:9-10). Truly Job was right to say his greatest comfort was that despite life's dangerous journey, he did not deny God. In the end God restored the fortunes of Job. It was Job who also said, *"I know that my redeemer lives, and that in the end he will stand on the earth. And after my skin has been destroyed, yet in my flesh I will see God; I myself will see him with my own eyes I, and not another. How my heart yearns within me"* (Job 19:25-27).

Take Away for Today

1. Can you say, like Job, that you are comforted by the fact that you have not cursed your heavenly Father, despite the pain?

2. If you cannot say this, are you prepared to ask for forgiveness and try again?

TRUE REPENTANCE MUST COME FROM WITHIN

When the king heard the woman's words, he tore his robes. As he went along the wall, the people looked, and they saw that, under his robes, he had sackcloth on his body (2 Kings 6:30).

THE king was wearing sackcloth beneath his royal robes. This king had a hate-love relationship with Prophet Elisha, but he was deeply spiritual person! He was mourning and praying for the siege on Jerusalem and the famine to come to an end.

His action is worthy of emulation. Although we may be fasting and praying within, we should on the outside wear our royal robes and smile and have a pleasant disposition.

Take Away for Today

1. When people see you, do they see gloom and doom or a smile and a pleasant attitude?
2. When you fast, do you tell others so they can think you are righteous and to be admired?

AN ILLUSION FROM GOD

But when they got up the next morning, the sun was shining across the water, making it appear red to the Moabites—like blood (2 Kings 3:22 NLT).

I N this instance, God confused the enemy! In the morning when the enemy woke they saw the miracle water and they thought it was the blood of the Israelites! Their human senses and perception failed them. After all, if there was no wind and no rain how can there be water? It was beyond human imagination. May God confuse the enemies of His plans for your life!

Take Away for Today

1. Are there plans you have that you should ask God to confuse the enemy about?
2. Can you go beyond your imagination into the realm of God to ask Him for protection from your enemy?

DON'T STOP PRAYING

Rejoice always, pray without ceasing, in everything give thanks; for this is the will of God in Christ Jesus for you (1 Thessalonians 5:16-18 NKJV).

HAVE you ever wondered how long you should continue to pray? Prayers never end because prayer is talking to God and is the opportunity to exchange human frailty for the supremacy and sovereignty of God in your situation. Prayer is a way of life! Also, Jesus *"told his disciples a parable to show them that they should always pray and not give up"* (Luke 18:1). Come to God expecting to receive from Him!

Take Away for Today

1. Do you still wonder how long you should continue to pray?
2. Is prayer a significant part of your lifestyle?
3. Is praying without ceasing a goal or an impossible task?

OVERCOME EVIL WITH GOOD

But I say to you, love your enemies, bless those who curse you, do good to those who hate you, and pray for those who spitefully use you and persecute you (Matthew 5:44).

CHRISTIANITY is based on solid principles of which the cross is the emblem. The cross is the emblem of human unfairness and wickedness, but it is also the truth of the forgiveness, benevolence, and mercies of God. This should be our inspiration—to overcome evil with goodness. Whatever good you make happen for others, God will make happen for you a thousand-fold!

Take Away for Today

1. "What goes around comes around" is a popular saying, how does it fit with today's Scripture verse.

2. Do your motives count when you are praying for those who have hurt you?

3. Does this verse inspire you to do good for others?

A CALL TO SPIRITUAL GROWTH

Solid food is for those who are mature, who through training have the skill to recognize the difference between right and wrong (Hebrews 5:10-14 NLT).

To grow means the process of increase or advancement. It requires patience, perseverance, and consistence. Often growth comes from what we are doing and practice makes perfect! In all aspects of life, this is a sure way to appropriate what Job said, *"And though your beginning was small, yet your latter end would greatly increase"* (Job 8:7 AMP). You will grow in God!

Take Away for Today

1. Are you eating spiritually solid food?
2. Do you have the skill to recognize the difference between right and wrong?
3. How eager are you to grow spiritually?

_____

_____

_____

YOUR DELIVERANCE HAS BEEN DECREED

The decision is announced by messengers, the holy ones declare the verdict, so that the living may know that the Most High is sovereign over all kingdoms on earth and gives them to anyone he wishes and sets over them the lowliest of people (Daniel 4:17).

THE true intent of some of the things you go through is to show the power of God through your circumstances and show that God rules in the affairs of all people.

God will grant you the garment of praise instead of the spirit of despair, you will be become the oak of righteousness and the display of His splendor.

Take Away for Today

1. Do you give God the glory in all things?
2. Do you wear the garment of praise rather than the spirit of despair?

THE CRY OF JABEZ

Jabez cried out to the God of Israel, "Oh, that you would bless me and enlarge my territory! Let your hand be with me, and keep me from harm so that I will be free from pain." And God granted his request (1 Chronicles 4:10).

THE teacher in the book of Ecclesiastes says bad people live long and good people die young and only God knows! Some are born into greatness and others into pain and misery, and still others have misery and an uncertain future thrown at them by circumstances beyond their control. There was a noble person who had misery thrown on him by the name given to him by his mother. Instead of blame shifting; Jabez reached to God who is able to stop anyone from falling. He cried out to God! If you must cry, then cry unto the Lord and make sure your cry is not amiss. Jabez cried out to the Lord and his cry was in line with the hand of God. May the Lord bless you, enlarge you, be with you, keep you, protect you, and remove your misery.

Take Away for Today

1. Are you a crier? Do you cry out to God or to others who may or may not have the right answers?

2. Are your cries in line with God's hand of love, grace, and mercy?

_____

_____

_____

EVERY ACT OF WICKEDNESS AGAINST YOU IS DISALLOWED

He aborts the schemes of conniving crooks, so that none of their plots come to term. He catches the know-it-alls in their conspiracies—all that intricate intrigue swept out with the trash! Suddenly they're disoriented, plunged into darkness; they can't see to put one foot in front of the other (Job 5:12-14 The Message).

N OTICE some great pivots in this passage:

- Conniving crooks will be disappointed and their plans aborted
- The conspiracies of the know-it-alls will be exposed and judged
- Every intricate intrigue will be washed away as trash
- Sudden confusion will come upon the enemy of God's plan in you
- Progress will elude your enemies

Take Away for Today

1. Have conniving crooks and know-it-alls made your life miserable at one time or another?
2. Will you stand firmly on this promise from God that wickedness will be disallowed in your life?

"GOD HAS COME TO HELP HIS PEOPLE!"

They were all filled with awe and praised God. "A great prophet has appeared among us," they said. "God has come to help his people" (Luke 16-17).

WHEN Jesus raised the dead son of the widow of Nain, He only touched the coffin, the procession stopped and funeral ended and celebration of life started because the son came to life. The people said, *"God has come to help His people!"* (see Luke 7:11-17).

Everything around you is subject to His touch. God has come to help you!

Take Away for Today

1. Have you felt the healing touch of God on your life? Physical, emotional, financial?

2. Are you forever grateful that God has come to help His people?

3. What testimony can you give today that proves He has helped you in some tangible way?

BLESSINGS—ONE THING FAST ON THE HEELS OF ANOTHER

"Yes indeed, it won't be long now." God's Decree. "Things are going to happen so fast your head will swim, one thing fast on the heels of the other. You won't be able to keep up. Everything will be happening at once and everywhere you look, blessings! Blessings like wine pouring off the mountains and hills. I'll make everything right again for my people" (Amos 9:13-15 The Message).

THIS is what is meant when you hear that "blessings overtake a person"! Imagine so many blessings that "your head will swim." This is your season of blessings. Blessings, blessings upon you!

Take Away for Today

1. Are you looking forward to seeing blessings everywhere you look?

2. Can you imagine blessings pouring off the mountains and hills like wine?

3. Write what comes to your mind after reading this Scripture passage in Amos.

RESTORE THE FORTUNE OF JACOB'S TENT

This is what the Lord says: "I will restore the fortunes of Jacob's tents and have compassion on his dwellings; the city will be rebuilt on her ruins, and the palace will stand in its proper place" (Jeremiah 30:18).

JACOB is the carrier of the promises of the Abrahamic covenant. The covenant of God has the peace and protection of God, but it also carries the benefits of the divine attributes of God such as God's mercies and compassion. God promises to restore those who are carriers of His covenant to their proper places!

Take Away for Today

1. Have you lost fortunes—relationships, friendships, respect, investments—that need to be restored?

2. Are there things or people who need to be set back into their proper places in your life?

_____

_____

_____

GOD IS NEAR

What other nation is so great as to have their gods near them the way the Lord our God is near us whenever we pray to him? And what other nation is so great as to have such righteous decrees and laws as this body of laws I am setting before you today? (Deuteronomy 4:7-8)

A S the people of God, we are privileged because the Lord is with us and He is also near us. The Bible says we are great to have God always on our side. The glory of His presence is reassuring, and in His presence also are His righteous decrees and laws to guide us—not oppress us.

Take Away for Today

1. Unlike other religions, followers of Christ have the assurance of a living, breathing God who lives within. Are you resting assured?

2. Are you basking in His presence?

THE LORD HELPS

Then Samuel took a stone and set it up between Mizpah and Shen. He named it Ebenezer, saying, "Thus far has the Lord helped us." So the Philistines were subdued and they stopped invading Israel's territory... (1 Samuel 7:12-13).

THE Lord will raise a rock of help and a rock of testimony called Ebenezer for you. The Lord is pleased and more than able to help you in your time of need. He is waiting for you to ask, to knock, to pray. He is eager for you to say, "Thus far has the Lord helped me." The Holy Spirit was sent to provide comfort and assistance—call on Him whenever you are in need.

Take Away for Today

1. Have you set up an Ebenezer stone signifying that the Lord has helped you thus far and that you are confident that He will help you throughout the remainder of your life?

2. Is God the first person you turn to for help?

DOUBLE BLESSINGS

Most blessed of sons is Asher; let him be favored by his brothers, and let him bathe his feet in oil. The bolts of your gates will be iron and bronze, and your strength will equal your days (Deuteronomy 33:24-25; also see Job 29:2-6 AMP).

BLESSINGS from God are always desirable. May we be receptive and appreciative of all His good gifts. I pray that you will be blessed with the blessing of Asher and twice the blessings of Job. The Lord is happy to bless us—let us receive with thanksgiving every gift He has for us.

Take Away for Today

1. Having blessings is nothing to be ashamed of. It is God's good pleasure to give you good things.

2. Do you sometimes feel guilty for having blessings when there are others who are without? Rather than feeling guilty, could you thank God for your situation and then share what you have with the less fortunate?

Reading the Bible in a Year: Ezekiel 1-3 and Hebrews 9.

A People Saved by God

Blessed are you, O Israel! Who is like you, a people saved by the Lord? He is your shield and helper and your glorious sword. Your enemies will cower before you, and you will tread on their heights (Deuteronomy 33:29).

THERE is no end to the Lord's compassion and protection. He reaches out from heaven to stop hearts from breaking, to keep war-mongering leaders from battling, to save the the drunks and addicted. But...because of the Fall, there is evil in the world and we must do what we can to stop the violence and the heartache. With Him as our shield and helper with a glorious sword, we are empowered to make the world a better place.

Take Away for Today

1. Are you ready to make a positive difference in your world?

2. Are you ready to see your enemies cower before you?

November 14

NO ONE WILL
STAND AGAINST YOU

No one will be able to stand up against you all the days of your life. As I was with Moses, so I will be with you; I will never leave you nor forsake you (Joshua 1:5).

THE phrase "I will never leave you nor forsake you" has sustained many Christians over many centuries. Those comforting words sink deep into hearts and minds and are available whenever feeling alone or abandoned. Being reassured by God in this manner gives every believer hope—a promise that will never be broken.

Take Away for Today

1. How many times have you relied on this promise of God?
2. Do you share this hope you have with others—people who have had their hearts and lives crushed by broken promises?

_____

_____

_____

EACH TO HIS OWN INHERITANCE

After Joshua had dismissed the Israelites, they went to take possession of the land, each to his own inheritance (Judges 2:6).

GOD gave the land of milk and honey to His people. They had been rescued from Egypt after many years of hard labor as slaves. They had no possessions as slaves—they were used and abused by their task masters, they had no identity. Now Joshua had led them into the Promised Land and they were taking possession, they were establishing their own inheritance for generations to come. As custodian of divine inheritance, always remember the future generation and do your best to make the world a better place for them.

Take Away for Today

1. Have you been a slave to your job, your religion, your insecurities?
2. Are you ready to take possession of a rich, full life of blessings in your Promised Land?

_____

_____

_____

GOOD CHANGES AND EVIL CHANGES

But Saul, who is also called Paul, filled with and controlled by the Holy Spirit, looked steadily at [Elymas] And said, You master in every form of deception and recklessness, unscrupulousness, and wickedness, you son of the devil, you enemy of everything that is upright and good, will you never stop perverting and making crooked the straight paths of the Lord and plotting against His saving purposes? (Acts 13:7-10 AMP).

THIS was the struggle between Paul filled with the Holy Spirit and Elymas filled with the spirit of his father—the devil. Just as the Holy Spirit can come upon people and change them for the good, we must be ever alert that wickedness, the sons of the devil, and the enemy of everything upright and good, is ever present to pervert and corrupt the path of Christians. We have to be like Paul who was filled with and controlled by the Holy Spirit so we can discern good from evil and fight the good fight.

Take Away for Today

1. How discerning are you regarding the evilness that tries to corrupt your steps?

2. What can you do to prevent wickedness from infiltrating your body, mind, and spirit?

By Nature Deserving of Wrath

...Like the rest, we were by nature deserving of wrath. But because of his great love for us, God, who is rich in mercy, made us alive with Christ even when we were dead in transgressions— it is by grace you have been saved (Ephesians 2:3-5).

W E are not where we are today because we have everything figured out. It is not by works we came to know God. Paul also wrote, *"For it is by grace you have been saved, through faith—and this is not from yourselves, it is the gift of God—not by works, so that no one can boast. For we are God's handiwork, created in Christ Jesus to do good works, which God prepared in advance for us to do"* (Eph. 2:8-10).

Take Away for Today

1. Although it is important to put your faith into action, what is more important?

2. How does God's infinite grace mesh with your vision of faith and deeds?

NO FOOLISHNESS

You foolish Galatians! Who has bewitched you? Before your very eyes Jesus Christ was clearly portrayed as crucified. I would like to learn just one thing from you: did you receive the Spirit by the works of the law, or by believing what you heard? Are you so foolish? After beginning by means of the Spirit, are you now trying to finish by means of the flesh?
(Galatians 3:1-3)

TO be called foolish is to be reprimanded. Paul was clearly upset with the Galatians for putting their faith in works rather than what they knew to be the truth of the Spirit. Works and faith must be partners, not exclusive. Always balance faith and works—one should complement the other in God's eyes.

Take Away for Today

1. Do you put works before faith or faith before works?
2. Do you have a balanced faith and works mindset?

_____

_____

_____

THERE IS A PRESCRIBED WAY

*Then David summoned Zadok and Abiathar the priests, and Uriel, Asaiah, Joel, Shemaiah, Eliel and Amminadab the Levites. He said to them, "You are the heads of the Levitical families; you and your fellow Levites are to consecrate yourselves and bring up the ark of the Lord, the God of Israel, to the place I have prepared for it. It was because you, the Levites, did not bring it up the first time that the Lord our God broke out in anger against us. **We did not inquire of him about how to do it in the prescribed way.**" So the priests and Levites consecrated themselves in order to bring up the ark of the Lord, the God of Israel. And the Levites carried the ark of God with the poles on their shoulders, as Moses had commanded in accordance with the word of the Lord (1 Chronicles 15:11-15).*

GOD created the heavens and the earth and set in place rules that will guide our way so there will be peace, joy, and harmony on earth. God has laws governing human existence on earth, and if we operate the systems in God's way, we will enjoy our life journey on earth. But if we neglect His rules and His prescribed way of doing things, pain, misery, and disappointment are bound to follow.

Here King David recalled their mistake of not following God's prescribed way and admonishes the people to follow the prescribed way of carrying the Ark of God on the shoulders of the Levites. Always seek God's prescribed way of doing things.

Take Away for Today

1. How can you be sure you are doing things in God's prescribed way?
2. Have you been neglecting His rules?

A GOOD WOMAN

A good woman is hard to find, and worth far more than diamonds. Her husband trusts her without reserve, and never has reason to regret it (Proverbs 31:10-11 The Message).

PROVERBS 31:10-31 reveals the attributes and characteristics of a "good wife." These aspects of a good wife can be analyzed, critiqued, and debated, but the bottom line is that a good woman is one who is honest, hard-working, and trustworthy. Many Christian women have earned this title and are blessings to their families. May we honor and cherish them as the gifts they are to us.

Take Away for Today

1. Would you consider yourself or your spouse a "good woman" or a "good man" based on the bottom line definition?

2. Do you daily give your "good woman" or "good man" the honor she or he deserves?

GODLY PARENTS: A SURE AND LASTING FOUNDATION

S AMUEL'S mother: *"I prayed for this child, and the Lord has granted me what I asked of him"* (1 Samuel 1:27). David for Solomon: *"'My son Solomon is young and inexperienced, and the house to be built for the Lord should be of great magnificence and fame and splendor in the sight of all the nations. Therefore I will make preparations for it.' So David made extensive preparations before his death"* (1 Chronicles 22:5). Job for his children: *"When a period of feasting had run its course, Job would make arrangements for them to be purified. Early in the morning he would sacrifice a burnt offering for each of them, thinking, 'Perhaps my children have sinned and cursed God in their hearts.' This was Job's regular custom"* (Job 1:5).

Godly parents are precious gifts from God.

Take Away for Today

1. Were you blessed with godly parents? How did their influence affect you?

2. Are, or were, your parents unbelievers? How did this affect your life growing up?

THE LORD TO THE RESCUE

How could one man chase a thousand, or two put ten thousand to flight, unless their Rock had sold them, unless the LORD had given them up? (Deuteronomy 32:30)

ONE man could not chase away 1,000 soldiers unless the Lord had something to do with it. It would be physically impossible for this to happen…yet it did. It did because the Lord made it happen. From Genesis to Revelation and until today and tomorrow, God makes the miraculous happen. We are privileged to be part of His family and to be privy to His miracles, signs, and wonders. The Lord will come to your rescue and chase a thousand before you.

Take Away for Today

1. Although you have probably not chased away 1,000 soldiers, how many times has God come to your rescue in other ways?

2. Have you witnessed miracles, signs, or wonders from God? What was your reaction?

SURROUNDED BY
A CLOUD OF WITNESSES

Therefore, since we are surrounded by such a great cloud of witnesses, let us throw off everything that hinders and the sin that so easily entangles. And let us run with perseverance the race marked out for us (Hebrews 12:1).

WE need to be aware of everything that may be hindering us and entangling us—keeping us from doing our best in representing the winners we are in Christ. May we be so wise as to ask for assistance from the great cloud of witnesses surrounding us, that they would point out to us our sin. Then when exposed, may we destroy it quickly and completely.

Take Away for Today

1. Are you running the best race possible?
2. Is there anything holding you back from winning the race in which God entered you?

THE SPIRIT GIVES LIFE

The Spirit gives life; the flesh counts for nothing. The words I have spoken to you—they are full of the Spirit and life (John 6:63).

WHEN we give in to the flesh and all the unpleasant and unhealthy consequences that ensue, we add another layer of death to our spirits and souls. The temporary pleasures that the worldly, fleshly desires quench are but wasted time and events. Only godly, spiritual words and activities will bring us life full of joy and love and peace.

Take Away for Today

1. Have you wasted days, weeks, years on satisfying desires that add up to nothing but bondage and death?

2. How much more full of life are you when you focus on His Word and His will?

FILLED WITH JOY

But let all who take refuge in you rejoice; let them sing joyful praises forever. Spread your protection over them, that all who love your name may be filled with joy. For you bless the godly, O Lord; you surround them with your shield of love (Psalm 5:11-12 NLT).

WHOEVER takes refuge in God can rejoice and sing His praises for an eternity. He will spread His protection of us and because we love His name, we can be filled with joy for an eternity. God blesses the godly and surrounds us with His shield of love. Hallelujah!

Take Away for Today

1. Are you habitually filled with joy?
2. Do you feel His protection spread over you with His shield of love?

THE TRUE REASON

Now my soul is troubled, and what shall I say? "Father, save me from this hour"? No, it was for this very reason I came to this hour (John 12:27).

WHEN Jesus was talking to His disciples, preparing them for His demise, He was very clear that yes, indeed, His soul was troubled, but even so He knew His ultimate reason, the true reason for being born on earth and living for 33 years among God's creations. Jesus wanted to fulfill His destiny of saving people from themselves and from the devil's wiles that lead to eternal damnation. Hallelujah! He was obedient even unto death.

Take Away for Today

1. Have you determined your destiny in Christ?
2. Are you moving forward to attaining the prize God has waiting for you?

DIFFICULT SITUATIONS EQUAL GREAT TESTIMONIES

"Come, let's sell him to the Ishmaelites and not lay our hands on him; after all, he is our brother, our own flesh and blood." His brothers agreed. So when the Midianite merchants came by, his brothers pulled Joseph up out of the cistern and sold him for twenty shekels of silver to the Ishmaelites, who took him to Egypt (Genesis 37:27-28).

STRONG situations give rise to great testimonies. Joseph was only guilty of being his father's favorite son—not of anything worthy of being sold into slavery. Yet, throughout all of the subsequent situations, he stayed hopeful and true to God Almighty. Let your present struggles turn out for your good—and for God's glory.

Take Away for Today

1. Do you have a great testimony (or more than one!) that came from a difficult situation?

2. Have you used the victorious testimony over your difficult situations to reveal the faithfulness and trustworthiness of God to others?

_____

_____

_____

THANK THE LORD

I will thank the Lord because he is just; I will sing praise to the name of the Lord Most High (Psalm 7:17 NLT).

WE have so very much to be thankful for—we could sing praises every day and every night for the remainder of our lives and it wouldn't be time enough. Thankfully we have eternity to sing His praises to His name. He is worthy to be thanked and praised for His mercy, goodness, faithfulness, grace, creation, parents, children, and love in sending His Son to earth to save us. I'm sure you can add others...

Take Away for Today

1. What are you most thankful for?
2. List as many things, people, events, etc. that come to mind for which you are thankful.

PICTURE LANGUAGE FROM GOD

I spoke to the prophets, gave them many visions and told parables through them (Hosea 12:10).

SYMBOLS and parables are vital components of God's language and communication with humankind. God uses symbols to package His messages so they leave lingering and graphic effects in our memory. They enable God to emphasize something while hiding other things for a future date. In this way God is able to bring the meanings of His messages in stages, in a way we are able to handle them at the appropriate time. God used the prophets of old to reveal what God had in His mind. God continues to use prophets today to reveal the same.

Take Away for Today

1. Have you encountered a prophet who had visions from God?

2. Do you believe that God still uses people as prophets to communicate with His people?

3. Have you received pictures—symbols and parables—from God that left permanent marks in your memory?

HUMANKIND WITHOUT GOD

A man without God is trusting in a spider's web. Everything he counts on will collapse (Job 8:14 The Living Bible).

THE present world we live in is a far cry from the perfect, peaceful world God created. God made the big and the small, the beautiful and the ugly, the strong and the feeble. He made them all. God put all He created under the dominion of humankind and blessed us to subdue any act of insurrection! This power is only available only if we obey His rules and depend and trust in Him. This is why the Bible says without God we are trusting in a spider web, which is bound to collapse.

Put your trust in God.

Take Away for Today

1. Are you trusting in the solid rock of God Almighty?
2. Are you trusting in a spider's web, which will eventually collapse?

DELIVERED FROM THE POWER OF THE GRAVE

I will deliver this people from the power of the grave; I will redeem them from death. Where, O death, are your plagues? Where, O grave, is your destruction?... (Hosea 13:14).

THIS passage of Scripture has been recited many times at many funerals and memorial services because it brings the mourners hope and comfort. It emphasizes that God has power over the grave. First Corinthians 15:54-55 (NKJV) says, *"So when this corruptible has put on incorruption, and this mortal has put on immortality, then shall be brought to pass the saying that is written: "Death is swallowed up in victory. O Death, where is your sting? O Hades, where is your victory?"*

Take Away for Today

1. Have you been comforted with these verses at the death of a loved one?

2. Are there other Scripture verses that you have found especially consoling? Write them here.

SHOWERS OF RIGHTEOUSNESS

Sow righteousness for yourselves, reap the fruit of unfailing love, and break up your unplowed ground; for it is time to seek the Lord, until he comes and showers his righteousness on you (Hosea 10:12).

AGAIN the Bible refers to sowing and reaping. This analogy is used frequently throughout the Bible because everyone can picture a seed being planted, a plant emerging from the ground, pushing up toward the light and life-giving water, and harvesting the fruit of the plant. Likewise, when we sow righteousness in ourselves by seeking the Light and the Living Water, we will reap the fruit of the Spirit! (See Galatians 5:22-23.)

Take Away for Today

1. How pleasant it is to think about being showered with His love and righteousness. Describe those showers over you.

2. Are you reaping righteousness from sowing goodness and mercy to others?

THE DAY OF THE LORD IS AT HAND

The days of punishment are coming, the days of reckoning are at hand. Let Israel know this. Because your sins are so many and your hostility so great, the prophet is considered a fool, the inspired person a maniac (Hosea 9:7).

MANY worldwide think sin and hostility are acceptable, that modern-day Christian prophets are imposters, and spiritually inspired people are maniacs. These beliefs seem to indicate that the days of punishment and days of reckoning are at hand according to Hosea 9:7. There are other indications that this season may be burgeoning. Let us prayerfully consider this possibility.

Take Away for Today

1. Do you think this verse is applicable to today's current events?

2. How close do you think we are to the "days of punishment" and the "days of reckoning"?

A JOYFUL SHOUT

Make a joyful shout to the Lord, all you lands! Serve the Lord with gladness; come before His presence with singing. Know that the Lord, He is God; it is He who has made us, and not we ourselves; we are His people and the sheep of His pasture (Psalm 100:1-3 NKJV).

WHAT an exuberant expression of happiness! We can almost hear the psalmist screaming this at the top of his lungs, wanting every shepherd, sheep, and creature within earshot to know the love he has for His Lord. This is how we should be—excited to share our love for God. Ready to SHOUT for joy and sing in His presence.

Take Away for Today

1. How excited are you to share the good news of God Almighty?
2. Have you ever SHOUTED for joy as did David?

SO THE LORD RELENTED

This is what the Sovereign Lord showed me: He was preparing swarms of locusts after the king's share had been harvested and just as the late crops were coming up. When they had stripped the land clean, I cried out, "Sovereign Lord, forgive! How can Jacob survive? He is so small!" So the Lord relented. "This will not happen," the Lord said (Amos 7:1-3).

AMOS tells us that he pleaded with the Lord, and the Lord relented. What a merciful God we serve that a mere mortal can approach the holy and all-powerful Lord of the universe and be heard—and this before Jesus came and gave us direct access to our heavenly Father through the Holy Spirit. So how more clearly are we now heard? Crystal clear from our mouths to God's ear!

Take Away for Today

1. Have you cried out to save a person, land, country?
2. Have you been saved from swarms of locusts because someone cried out for you?

Your Prayer Is Heard

But the angel said to him, "Do not be afraid, Zacharias, for **your prayer is heard;** *and your wife Elizabeth will bear you a son, and you shall call his name John. And you will have joy and gladness, and many will rejoice at his birth. For he will be great in the sight of the Lord, and shall drink neither wine nor strong drink. He will also be filled with the Holy Spirit, even from his mother's womb. And he will turn many of the children of Israel to the Lord their God (Luke 1:13-16 NKJV).*

THE Lord sent an angel to tell Zacharias that he and his wife, Elizabeth, would have a son—who became John the Baptist. John was a great man of God who baptized Jesus and brought many people to the saving grace of their heavenly Father. We need not be afraid or worried that God isn't listening to our prayers—He is listening and He will answer our prayers.

Take Away for Today

1. Are there times when you doubt God is listening to you?
2. When your prayers are not answered immediately, do you doubt God heard you?

RESTORE THE SPIRIT OF PRAISE

*In that day I will restore David's fallen shelter—I will repair
its broken walls and restore its ruins—and will rebuild it as
it used to be* (Amos 9:11).

DAVID was known to praise God in times of troubles and times
of joyous victory. David was a man of praise. Amos is telling
us that David's fallen shelter represents the fallen state of our times,
which includes the lack of praise and honor of God. May we join
in the Lord's desire to restore the Spirit of Praise throughout all the
lands.

Take Away for Today

1. God is worthy to be praised—are you fulfilling His
   desire?
2. Will you help repair the broken walls and ruins of the
   Spirit of Praise within the church?

OVERTAKEN BY BLESSINGS

How precious it is, Lord, to realize that you are thinking about me constantly! I can't even count how many times a day your thoughts turn toward me. And when I waken in the morning, you are still thinking of me! (Psalm 139:17-18 The Living Bible)

DAVID was constantly connected to God—when asleep and awake. God was ever watchful of David, and David felt His presence throughout the day and night. Their thoughts intermingled and they were one with each other—enjoying moments of intimacy and love. God thinks of us as well; He knows every thought we think and every desire we have. What a great God we serve!

Take Away for Today

1. Write this passage of Scripture in your own words, describing your feelings about God's ever watchful eye.

2. Are you overtaken by blessings with this realization that God is constantly thinking about you?

HALLELUJAH!

Hallelujah! Yes, praise the Lord! Praise him in his Temple and in the heavens he made with mighty power. Praise him for his mighty works. Praise his unequaled greatness. Praise him with the trumpet and with lute and harp. Praise him with the drums and dancing. Praise him with stringed instruments and horns. Praise him with the cymbals, yes, loud clanging cymbals. Let everything alive give praises to the Lord! You praise him! Hallelujah! (Psalm 150:1-6 The Living Bible)

IN every way we are to praise the Lord. The psalmist is very clear that we should praise God by singing, dancing, playing instruments and even LOUD clanging cymbals. Many churches today are rising to this admonition and including more than traditional organ music. Many congregants are seen dancing in the aisles and clapping their hands as the Spirit moves them. Sometimes "Hallelujah!" is shouted when people are overcome with His unequaled greatness and mighty power.

Take Away for Today

1. How demonstrative are you during worship and praise time in your church?
2. Do you feel free to express your praise openly?

SEARCH ME, LEAD ME

Search me, O God, and know my heart; test my thoughts.
Point out anything you find in me that makes you sad, and
lead me along the path of everlasting life (Psalm 139:23-24
The Living Bible).

A S we come to the close of this year and think back to each day's blessings revealed through the Word of God, let us ask Him to search our hearts, test our thoughts, and point out anything that makes Him sad. Then let us rid ourselves of whatever He reveals to us and allow Him to lead us into abundant life on earth and everlasting life to come.

Take Away for Today

1. Today are you willing to open your heart, soul, mind, and body so He can take total control?

2. Are there things within you that make God sad? What are you going to do about them?

December 11

Two Walking Together

*Do two walk together unless they have agreed to do so? Does
a lion roar in the thicket when it has no prey? Does it growl in
its den when it has caught nothing? (Amos 3:3-4)*

BELIEVERS agreeing to walk together brings companionship.
With companionship people grow and learn and are encouraged. With encouragement relationships blossom and bloom and fill
the air with the fragrance of the Lord's sweet goodness. It is good to
join ourselves with others of like mind so we can feed off each other
and be nourished.

Take Away for Today

1. Are you a loner or a crowd pleaser?
2. Do you enjoy the company of other believers?
3. Is it hard for you to relate to other believers? Why is
    that?

_____

_____

_____

WE WILL POSSESS OUR INHERITANCE

God's Judgment Day is near for all the godless nations. As you have done, it will be done to you. ...But not so on Mount Zion—there's respite there! A safe and holy place! The family of Jacob will take back their possessions from those who took them from them (Obadiah 1:15-17 The Message).

MOUNT Zion is a safe and holy place. There the family of Jacob, of Abraham, will repossess their inheritance and live safely and peacefully. That region of the world is in constant turmoil, but God says there will be safety for His people there one day. Constant prayers need to be offered to God that peace will come in His timing and in His perfect will.

Take Away for Today

1. Do you keep Israel and the people who live there in your prayers for peace and safety?
2. Do you believe that peace is possible between Israel and the surrounding countries in your lifetime?

_____

_____

_____

THE ANGEL SAID

*Now in the sixth month the angel Gabriel was sent by God
to a city of Galilee named Nazareth, to a virgin betrothed
to a man whose name was Joseph, of the house of David.
The virgin's name was Mary. And having come in, the angel
said to her, "Rejoice, highly favored one, the Lord is with you;
blessed are you among women!"* (Luke 1:26-28 NKJV)

ANGELS play important roles throughout the Bible. I venture to
say that this angel, Gabriel, was extremely honored to have been
chosen to bring the message to the mother of Jesus. This angel had
the privilege of telling Mary that she would bring into the world the
Savior, Christ the Lord, who would lead her people into an unknown,
beautiful world of miracles and wonders.

Take Away for Today

1. Write a few sentences using your spiritual imagination
    that describes what the angel Gabriel may have been
    thinking as he approached Mary to tell her the news.

2. Have angels played a role in your life? Bringing mes-
    sages from the Lord?

_____

_____

_____

WHEN LIFE EBBS AWAY

*When my life was ebbing away, I remembered you, Lord, and
my prayer rose to you, to your holy temple (Jonah 2:7).*

FROM an impending birth discussed yesterday, we go to Jonah
and his dilemma. As Mary sought the Lord about what was said
to her, Jonah "remembered" the Lord and prayed to Him. As he felt
his life slowly draining from him as he was in the belly of the whale,
Jonah turned to God, knowing that He would save him. God gives us
strength to face life and death.

Take Away for Today

1. Do you sometimes feel life ebbing away? Do you remember the Lord and pray?

2. Can you, do you depend on and trust in God to give you strength for every challenge?

SENTIMENT VERSUS OBEDIENCE

"Pick me up and throw me into the sea," he replied, "and it will become calm. I know that it is my fault that this great storm has come upon you." Instead, the men did their best to row back to land. But they could not, for the sea grew even wilder than before. Then they cried out to the Lord, "Please, Lord, do not let us die for taking this man's life. Do not hold us accountable for killing an innocent man, for you, Lord, have done as you pleased." Then they took Jonah and threw him overboard, and the raging sea grew calm. At this the men greatly feared the Lord, and they offered a sacrifice to the Lord and made vows to him (Jonah 1:12-17).

JONAH knew that his disobedience to God was causing the fierce storm. He knew that he must sacrifice himself to save the others—the innocent. Although the men did not want to toss Jonah overboard to a sure death, they obeyed Jonah's wishes and over he went. These were God-fearing men who prayed that it would be well with them. Sometimes we need to do the right thing although it seems otherwise—God knows our motives, trust Him!

Take Away for Today

1.   Is sentimentality a stronger motive than obedience at times?

2.   Is doing the right thing always the best thing in your mind?

SWALLOWED

Then God assigned a huge fish to swallow Jonah. Jonah was in the fish's belly three days and nights (Jonah 1:17).

NO doubt Jonah was thrashing around in the sea, praying, and possibly thinking that he was experiencing his last breaths. Although the storm had calmed, there he was in the vast sea filled with all types of creatures. When a huge fish swallowed Jonah, he prayed and God told the fish to vomit Jonah onto the seashore. When we have been disobedient or disrespectful to God, He may cause us to be shut up in a whale—a place where we can focus on our predicament and come to terms with what is really important.

Take Away for Today

1. Has God ever had to place you in the belly of a fish to get you to come to your senses?

2. Have you ever felt as if you had been vomited out into life after coming to your senses?

_____

_____

_____

ONE OF THE GREATEST EVANGELISTIC MESSAGES EVER

Then the word of the Lord came to Jonah a second time: "Go to the great city of Nineveh and proclaim to it the message I give you." Jonah obeyed the word of the Lord and went to Nineveh. ...proclaiming, "Forty more days and Nineveh will be overthrown." The Ninevites believed God. A fast was proclaimed, and all of them, from the greatest to the least, put on sackcloth. ...When God saw what they did and how they turned from their evil ways, he relented and did not bring on them the destruction he had threatened (Jonah 3:1-10).

GOD is the God of second chances! After Jonah's failure, God gave the anointing, the message, and the hearts of the people so he was able to give one of the greatest evangelistic messages ever! A great and merciful God approached Jonah a second time and told him to preach the good news to the Ninevites. This time, rather than running away, he obeyed God and all the people turned from their evil ways and God spared their lives. At first Jonah was afraid to go to Nineveh, but after the storm and the whale, he chose to obey the next time God asked. We must not be as stubborn as Jonah. Let us determine to hear and then act on God's word to us.

Take Away for Today

1. When we obey God, lives are saved. Yes?
2. Are you stubborn at times? Have you pretended not to hear God just so you don't have to obey Him?

REFUGE
IN TIMES OF TROUBLE

Whatever they plot against the Lord he will bring to an end; trouble will not come a second time. The Lord is good, a refuge in times of trouble. He cares for those who trust in him
(Nahum 1:9,7).

WE all need a place of refuge in times of trouble. We may be in a crowded store or business office when we get bad news, but we can seek refuge in the God who lives within us. We may be involved in an accident with no one we know around, but our dearest and closest Friend is always with us. No matter the circumstances, the Lord is our refuge and ever present strength in times of trouble.

Take Away for Today

1. Do you seek refuge in God rather than outside forces?
2. Do you count on Him first?

THE GLORY OF THE LORD

*For the earth will be filled with the knowledge of the **glory of the Lord** as the waters cover the sea. The Lord is in his holy temple; let all the earth be silent before him* (Habakkuk 2:14,20).

REVELATION 21:21-17 (The Message) also speaks of the glory of the Lord: "The main street of the City was pure gold, translucent as glass. ...The City doesn't need sun or moon for light. God's Glory is its light, the Lamb its lamp! The nations will walk in its light and earth's kings bring in their splendor. Its gates will never be shut by day, and there won't be any night. They'll bring the glory and honor of the nations into the City. ...Only those whose names are written in the Lamb's Book of Life will get in." What a glorious picture these verses paint for us!

Take Away for Today

1. How would you describe the "glory of the Lord"?
2. Are you ready to bask in His glory and walk on streets of pure gold?

SEEK THE LORD, RIGHTEOUSNESS, HUMILITY

Seek the Lord [inquire for Him, inquire of Him, and require Him as the foremost necessity of your life], all you humble of the land who have acted in compliance with His revealed will and have kept His commandments; seek righteousness, seek humility [inquire for them, require them as vital]. It may be you will be hidden in the day of the Lord's anger (Zephaniah 2:3 AMP).

IN Matthew 6:33 we are told to seek first the Kingdom of God, and in Zephaniah we are told to seek the Lord, righteousness, and humility. A recurring theme throughout the Bible is to "seek," which means we are not to sit back and relax and let the world pass us by. No. We are to be actively seeking more and more of Christ and His Kingdom. When we seek we will find—but there is always more to discover. Keep seeking!

Take Away for Today

1. Are you actively seeking the Lord? His Kingdom? Righteousness? Humility?

2. After a revelation is discovered, do you keep seeking for more?

FEAR NO HARM

The Lord has taken away your punishment, he has turned back your enemy. The Lord, the King of Israel, is with you; never again will you fear any harm (Zephaniah 3:15).

THE Lord has taken away our punishment, turning back the enemy—at the cross. Never again do we have to fear—our Lord is with us always, until the end of days and into eternity. Because of Jesus, we can rest assured that our future is secure and our eternal rest procured.

Take Away for Today

1. Fear is not from God—can you rest easy each night knowing that?
2. Are you confident of your final resting place?

THE WORD OF GOD CAME

...the word of God came to John the son of Zacharias in the wilderness. And he went into all the region around the Jordan, preaching a baptism of repentance for the remission of sins, as it is written in the book of the words of Isaiah the prophet, saying: "The voice of one crying in the wilderness: 'Prepare the way of the Lord; make His paths straight. Every valley shall be filled and every mountain and hill brought low; the crooked places shall be made straight and the rough ways smooth; and all flesh shall see the salvation of God'"
(Luke 3:2-6 NKJV).

THE word of God came to John, and the Word of God came to the world—to us—in the form of the Son of God. John prepared the way for the Messiah, the salvation of God. Many accepted John's proclamations, many today accept—but many do not. We need to do our best to follow John's example of crying in the wilderness.

Take Away for Today

1. In this age of mass communication, are you taking advantage of spreading "the Word" whenever possible?
2. List five ways you can share "the Word" with others today.

BAPTIZED WITH THE HOLY SPIRIT AND FIRE

But John intervened: "I'm baptizing you here in the river. The main character in this drama, to whom I'm a mere stagehand, will ignite the kingdom life, a fire, the Holy Spirit within you, changing you from the inside out. He's going to clean house— make a clean sweep of your lives. He'll place everything true in its proper place before God; everything false he'll put out with the trash to be burned (Luke 3:16-17 The Message).

JOHN always gave Jesus "top billing." John knew who Jesus was— the Messiah, Christ the Lord, the Son of God—and he wanted to make sure that everyone knew the difference between Jesus and himself, Jesus' cousin. The Message version of this familiar verse expounds on the changes that will take place when you experience the baptism of the Holy Spirit.

Take Away for Today

1. Have you experienced the Holy Spirit baptism?
2. If yes, were you changed from the inside out?

FROM THIS DAY ON

*From this day on, from this twenty-fourth day of the ninth
month, give careful thought to the day when the foundation
of the Lord's temple was laid. Give careful thought: Is there
yet any seed left in the barn? Until now, the vine and the fig
tree, the pomegranate and the olive tree have not borne fruit.
"From this day on I will bless you"* (Haggai 2:18-19).

FROM the day Jesus was born, the world became a different place.
From the time of the Fall of humankind until the day of Jesus'
birth there was no lasting, eternal fruit. Only the Son of God emerging on the scene brought blessings and glory and power into the
fallen world. From that day on God provided our salvation. Thanks
be to God!

Take Away for Today

1. Do you remember the day you were born again?
2. What were those feelings like and do you revive those
   feelings frequently?

CHRIST IS BORN

Joseph also went up from Galilee, out of the city of Nazareth, into Judea, to the city of David, which is called Bethlehem, because he was of the house and lineage of David, to be registered with Mary, his betrothed wife, who was with child. So it was, that while they were there, the days were completed for her to be delivered. And she brought forth her firstborn Son, and wrapped Him in swaddling cloths, and laid Him in a manger, because there was no room for them in the inn (Luke 2:4-7 NKJV).

THIS is the day we celebrate the birth of Jesus. The story is so familiar that we may have it memorized. This is good. This is right. We should know this story by heart and share it with everyone who will listen. This is the beginning of a world filled with God's love—"For God so loved the world that He gave His only begotten Son so that whosoever believeth in Him should not perish but have everlasting life."

Take Away for Today

1. How many times have you recited this story to yourself, your family, your children...strangers?

2. Do you believe that this story about Jesus' birth never gets old and that it becomes fresh each time you tell it?

Reading the Bible in a Year: Haggai and Revelation 16.

THE ANGELS AND THE SHEPHERDS

And suddenly there was with the angel a multitude of the heavenly host praising God and saying: "Glory to God in the highest, and on earth peace, goodwill toward men!" So it was, when the angels had gone away from them into heaven, that the shepherds said to one another, "Let us now go to Bethlehem and see this thing that has come to pass, which the Lord has made known to us." And they came with haste and found Mary and Joseph, and the Babe lying in a manger. Now when they had seen Him, they made widely known the saying which was told them concerning this Child. And all those who heard it marveled at those things which were told them by the shepherds (Luke 2:13-18 NKJV).

ANGELS again. This time they were praising God and celebrating the birth of His Son, and alerting the shepherds of the miracle. The shepherds left their sheep and went into the little town of Bethlehem to see Jesus. They knew they had seen the Messiah and told whoever would listen about the good news.

Take Away for Today

1. Are you as excited to sing for joy as the angels were?
2. Are you as awestruck as the shepherds that you will make "widely known the saying which was told them concerning this Child"?

HIS NAME WAS CALLED JESUS

But Mary kept all these things and pondered them in her heart. ...And when eight days were completed for the circumcision of the Child, His name was called Jesus, the name given by the angel before He was conceived in the womb (Luke 2:19-21 NKJV).

MARY remembered what the angel Gabriel had told her before the Holy Spirit came upon her. The Child's name was Jesus and she knew He was destined for great, yet terrible things. His mother loved Him and held Him close to her heart all of the days of His life. Mary thought about His future, as all parents think about their children's life. When we know that our children are ultimately in the Lord's hands, we can rest assured that He will watch over them day and night.

Take Away for Today

1. Do you have a child or children who keep you up with worry at night?

2. Can you trust God enough, like Mary had to, to turn your children over to God, knowing that He will watch over them?

_____

_____

_____

JESUS—OUR SALVATION

And behold, there was a man in Jerusalem whose name was Simeon.... And it had been revealed to him by the Holy Spirit that he would not see death before he had seen the Lord's Christ. So he came by the Spirit into the temple. And when the parents brought in the Child Jesus...he took Him up in his arms and blessed God and said: "Lord, now You are letting Your servant depart in peace, according to Your word; for my eyes have seen Your salvation which You have prepared before the face of all peoples, a light to bring revelation to the Gentiles, and the glory of Your people Israel" (Luke 2:25-32 NKJV).

L ED by the Holy Spirit, Simeon went to the temple and there he saw Jesus, the Christ Child. He held Him and thanked God for allowing him to see the salvation of the world before dying. Simeon acknowledged that the Lord had set in motion a plan to redeem His wayward children—through Jesus the Savior of the world.

Take Away for Today

1. When the time comes, can you "depart in peace" knowing that you have seen your salvation?

2. Have you thanked God today for the gift of His Son?

THE GRACE OF GOD

*So when they had performed all things according to the law of the
Lord, they returned to Galilee, to their own city, Nazareth. And
the Child grew and became strong in spirit, filled with wisdom;
and the grace of God was upon Him* (Luke 2:39-40 NKJV).

THE grace of God was upon Jesus as He grew up. The grace of
God is also upon us as we welcome Him into our daily and
nightly lives. The grace of God is what keeps us going through thick
and thin, through joy and sadness, and through life and approaching
death. The grace of God is the Lord's way of telling us that we are
truly His children and He loves us no matter what.

Take Away for Today

1. Have you had to depend on God's grace to get you
   through some tough times?

2. Do you depend on the fact that God's grace never ends?
   There will always be enough every time you ask?

_____

_____

_____

GOD IS WELL PLEASED

Now when all the people were baptized, and when Jesus also had been baptized, and [while He was still] praying, the [visible] heaven was opened and the Holy Spirit descended upon Him in bodily form like a dove, and a voice came from heaven, saying, You are My Son, My Beloved! In You I am well pleased and find delight! (Luke 3:21-22 AMP)

JOHN the Baptist was baptizing those who believed—then along came Jesus. John baptized Him and while Jesus was praying to His Father, heaven opened and the Holy Spirit, like a dove, came down onto Him. Then a voice from heaven declared for all to hear, "You are My beloved Son; in You I am well pleased." Hallelujah! May we hear God say that He is well pleased with us as well. We are on earth to serve Him—may we do so with joy and thankful hearts.

Take Away for Today

1. Most days, do you believe God is pleased with you?
2. Why do you think God chose a dove to deliver His Holy Spirit upon Jesus?

ABUNDANT LIFE—YEAR AFTER YEAR

*...I have come that they may have life, and that they may
have it more abundantly* (John 10:10).

ACCORDING to this verse in John, Jesus said He came to earth to give us abundant life. His birth, life, death, and resurrection were planned by God before the beginning. His is our life and in Him we have our being, our dreams, our destiny. Let us spend each moment of our life willing to obey and reap the harvest He has sown for us from the beginning of time. Let us choose to dedicate the New Year to the One who holds every moment of every year in the palm of His able hands.

Take Away for Today

1. Do you usually make New Year resolutions?
2. Has God laid a resolution or two on your heart?

A Place of Love and Refreshment
At the Heartbeat of
Aberdeen

THE FATHER'S HOUSE
Spreading the love of the Father abroad

Unveiling the Treasure in earthen vessels

www.the-fathers-house.org.uk

CONTACT INFORMATION

For additional copies of this book and other products from Cross House Books, contact: sales@crosshousebooks.co.uk.

Please visit our Website for product updates and news at www.crosshousebooks.co.uk.

OTHER INQUIRIES

CROSS HOUSE BOOKS
Christian Book Publishers
245 Midstocket Road, Aberdeen, AB15 5PH, UK

info@crosshousebooks.co.uk
publisher@crosshousebooks.co.uk

"The entrance of Your Word brings light."

**Do you want to become a published author
and get your book distributed worldwide
by major book stores?**

Contact:
admin@crosshousebooks.co.uk
www.crosshousebooks.co.uk.
or write to
CROSS HOUSE BOOKS
245 Midstocket Road, Aberdeen, AB15 5PH, UK

NEW TITLES FROM
CROSS HOUSE BOOKS

Times of Refreshing Volume 2

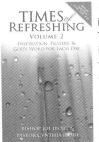

Times of Refreshing Volume 2 gives readers the ability to tap in to daily supernatural experiences! As with Times of Refreshing Volume 1, Volume 2 overflows with inspiring messages, comforting prayers, and Scriptures that bring His presence home. These daily boosts of God's love are just what the Divine Doctor ordered for a healthy mind, body, and spirit. Each page includes a Scripture and God-given message, as well as space for interactive exchanges of the reader's written word with His. An added bonus is a listing of Scriptures to read the Bible in a year. Prophetic Prayer Points conclude this volume of encouraging and motivating messages of daily living the supernatural, victorious life in God's Kingdom.

The Enemy Called Worry

Worry gives birth to many sins and affects a person's spiritual development and physical health. There is a way to eliminate worry from your life and move forward into your God-given destiny. This book gives you every weapon needed to proclaim victory over The Enemy Called Worry!

Revelations Training Manual

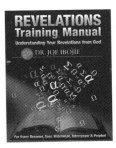

Revelations Training Manual takes you into the depths of God's holiness and desire to communicate with His children. It is possible to understand your dreams and revelations from God—and with the wisdom shared in this manual, your spiritual questions will be answered.

BOOKS BY DR. JOE IBOJIE

Destined for the Top

Destined for the Top presents simple and proven success-ful answers to life's most complex questions. Divided into two parts—Life Issues and Family Issues—you can be at the top of your game in every aspect of your life by know-ing what and who to avoid during your journey to the top. Through an added feature of thought-provoking ques-tions at the end of each chapter, you will learn how to strengthen your spirit, invest in your potential, and realize how fickle your feelings really are. You will discover how God's wisdom and love through you propels you toward fulfilling your destiny!

Times of Refreshing Volume 1

Times of Refreshing allows you to tap in to daily super-natural experiences! Overflowing with inspiring messages, comforting prayers, and Scriptures that bring His presence to you, these daily boosts of God's love are just what the Doctor ordered for a healthy mind, body, and spirit. Best-selling author and Pastor Bishop Joe Ibojie and Pastor Cynthia Ibojie bring 365 days of hope and refreshment into your personal space.

How to Live the Supernatural Life in the Here and Now—BEST SELLER

Are you ready to stop living an ordinary life? You were meant to live a supernatural life! God intends us to experi-ence His power every day! In *How to Live the Supernatural Life in the Here and Now* you will learn how to bring the supernatural power of God into everyday living. Finding the proper balance for your life allows you to step into the supernatural and to move in power and authority over everything around you. Dr. Joe Ibojie, an experienced pas-tor and prolific writer, provides practical steps and instruction that will help you live a life of spiritual harmony.

Dreams and Visions Volume 1—BEST SELLER

Dreams and Visions presents sound scriptural principles and practical instructions to help you understand dreams and visions. The book provides readers with the necessary understanding to approach dreams and visions by the Holy Spirit through biblical illustrations, understanding of the meaning of dreams and prophetic symbolism, and by exploring the art of dream interpretation according to ancient methods of the Bible.

Korean translations:
Dreams and Visions Volume 1

Italian translation:
Dreams and Visions Volume 1

Dreams and Visions Volume 2—NEW

God speaks to you through dreams and visions. Do you want to know the meaning of your dreams? Do you want to know what He is telling and showing you? Now you can know! *Dreams and Visions Volume 2* is packed full of exciting and Bible-guided ways to discover the meaning of your God-inspired, dreamy nighttime adventures and your wide-awake supernatural experiences!

Illustrated Bible-Based Dictionary of Dream Symbols—BEST SELLER

Illustrated Bible-Based Dictionary of Dream Symbols is much more than a book of dream symbols. This book is a treasure chest, loaded down with revelation and the hidden mysteries of God that have been waiting since before the foundation of the earth to be uncovered. Whether you use this book to assist in interpreting your dreams or as an additional resource for your study of the Word of God, you will find it a welcome companion.

EXPANDED AND ENRICHED WITH EXCITING NEW CONTENT

Bible-Based Dictionary of Prophetic Symbols for Every Christian

The most comprehensive, illustrated Bible-based dictionary of prophetic and dream symbols ever compiled is contained in this one authoritative book! *The Bible-Based Dictionary of Prophetic Symbols for Every Christian* is a masterpiece that intelligently and understandably bridges the gap between prophetic revelation and application—PLUS it includes the expanded version of the best-selling *Illustrated Bible-Based Dictionary of Dream Symbols*.

The Justice of God: Victory in Everyday Living

Only once in a while does a book bring rare insight and godly illumination to a globally crucial subject. This book is one of them! A seminal work from a true practitioner, best-selling author, and leader of a vibrant church, Dr. Joe Ibojie brings clarity and a hands-on perspective to the Justice of God. *The Justice of God* reveals: How to pull down your blessings; How to work with angels; The power and dangers of prophetic acts drama, and so much more!

The Watchman: The Ministry of the Seer in the Local Church

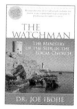

The ministry of the watchman in a local church is possibly one of the most common and yet one of the most misunderstood ministries in the Body of Christ. Over time, the majority of these gifted people have been driven into reclusive lives because of relational issues and confusion surrounding their very vital ministry in the local church.

The Final Frontiers—Countdown to the Final Showdown

The Final Frontiers—Countdown to the Final Showdown peers profoundly into the future. It expertly explores the emerging cosmic involvement of the seemingly docile elements of nature and their potential to completely alter the ways of warfare. Christians must not allow the things that are supposed to bless them to become instruments of judgment or punishment. *The Final Frontiers* provides you with a practical approach to the changing struggles that confront humanity now and in your future.

ADDITIONAL TITLES FROM CROSS HOUSE BOOKS

Growing God's Kingdom

Written by an experienced Bible scholar and beloved pastor, the insights and depth of God's word is thoughtfully shared so that newborn Christians and mature believers alike can understand and appreciate. Prefaced with an intriguing prophecy, *Growing God's Kingdom* contains practical principles that reveal the importance of God's mandate to share the gospel. You will learn about being mentored and mentoring those next in line to inherit God's riches.

40 Names of the Holy Spirit

The names of God represent a deliberate *invitation to you* to take advantage of what God can and wants to be in your life. Whatever you call Him is what He will become to you. Do you know all of His names? How much deeper would you like to know the Comforter? You will learn: Seven Symbols of the Holy Spirit; Names of the Holy Spirit; Seven Things *Not* to Do to the Holy Spirit; Twentyfold Relationship with the Holy Spirit; Fourfold Presence of the Holy Spirit; Seven Keys to Receiving the Holy Spirit Baptism—and much more!

TITLES SOON TO BE RELEASED

How You Can Live an Everyday Supernatural Life

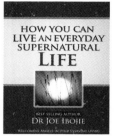

This comprehensive manual is the perfect training ground for every believer! Filled with practical and easy-to-implement ways to achieve a supernatural lifestyle, readers can immediately put into practice the God-given advice, insights, and revelations. Essential keys are presented that open the doors into a realm of divine and intimate relationship with God. He welcomes all to enjoy daily spiritual and physical miracles, signs, and wonders—naturally in the supernatural. Senior Pastor Joe Ibojie is a worldwide Bible and prophetic teacher.

From Rogue to Revivalist

From Rogue to Revivalist is the fascinating, true story of a young man whose early life resembles nothing of his later life—although each stage was preparing him for the miracles God performs through him today. Set in exotic and not-so-exotic countries worldwide, the journey leads readers into mesmerizing and shocking scenes that prove God's ultimate protection for all who call upon His name. Laced with dozens of personal testimonies from people healed by God's touch, this book is sure to impact every reader. Pastor Kul Bal travels worldwide as a healing revivalist.